Monica Russel is a qualified teacher and art therapist, and has worked in schools, further education and mental health services. In 2009, she set up a knitting and cake-stand making business using her creative skills. Monica designs all her own patterns and sells her knitting kits, which use only natural fibres, through her website. She attends many craft and knitting fairs and loves craft challenges. Since setting up her craft business, she has had patterns featured in knitting magazines and books. Her work can be seen at www.theknitknacks.co.uk

Head-to-Toe
WINTER KNITS

First published in 2018

Search Press Limited
Wellwood, North Farm Road,
Tunbridge Wells, Kent TN2 3DR

Reprinted 2019, 2020, 2021

Head-to-Toe Winter Knits uses material from
the following books by Monica Russel in the
Twenty to Make series published by Search Press:

Knitted Boot Cuffs, 2012
Easy Knitted Scarves, 2013
Knitted Wrist Warmers, 2014
Knitted Headbands, 2015
Knitted Snoods, 2016
Knitted Hats, 2017

ISBN: 978-1-78221-608-7

The Publishers and author can accept no responsibility
for any consequences arising from the information,
advice or instructions given in this publication.

Readers are permitted to reproduce any of the items in
this book for their personal use, or for the purpose of
selling for charity, free of charge and without the prior
permission of the Publishers. Any use of the items for
commercial purposes is not permitted without the prior
permission of the Publishers.

Suppliers
If you have difficulty in obtaining any of the materials
and equipment mentioned in this book, then please visit
the Search Press website for details of suppliers:
www.searchpress.com

You are invited to visit the author's website at:
theknitknacks.co.uk

Monica Russel

Head-to-Toe
WINTER KNITS
100 quick and easy accessories to knit

Search Press

Contents

Introduction

If you love knitting, this is the book for you!

Featuring 100 designs from six of Monica Russel's books in the *Twenty to Make* series, it is packed full of quick and easy patterns. There are lots of projects that will appeal to competent beginners and more advanced knitters alike and they are all made in lovely natural yarns with a wide range of colours and designs.

The range of projects includes knitted beanies, scarves, headbands, wrist warmers, snoods or infinity scarves and boot cuffs, so there is something here for everyone. Quick to make and stylish, there is no excuse for not being warm and snuggly with these winter knits!

There is a short section on knitting know-how at the beginning of the book, together with a list of useful knitting abbreviations that are used in the patterns. Every one of these beautiful knitted items will make lovely, personalized gifts for family and friends and they include knits for men, women and one or two for children. If you are an experienced knitter, you can adjust the sizing as you wish. The techniques used include cable stitch, lace and intarsia.

Hand knit your own fabulous winter accessories and match them to your preferred colour scheme. Whatever the occasion, there is a wealth of inspiration here with projects that will make the perfect gifts for birthdays, anniversaries, Valentine's Day and Christmas and will become an essential part of your winter wardrobe.

Happy knitting!

Knitting know-how

General notes

The sizes of the items in the projects are for guidance and many of them can be adapted to suit your taste, making them suitable for all sizes. As far as the scarves are concerned, for example, exact sizes are not needed to get a perfect end result, so you can repeat sections or add or remove rows to make them longer or shorter as you wish, unless they have shaping; in this case, follow the pattern instructions.

Yarn

All the projects in this book have been knitted in natural fibres. I chose the yarns for their luxurious feel and quality, but any comparable weight yarn can be substituted. It is advisable to check the yardage of the yarn that you buy against the ones used in the patterns to ensure that you have enough to finish your item.

Yarns are available in balls, skeins and hanks. Balls and skeins of yarn are ready-wound so that you can immediately knit from them, while hanks are coils of yarn that need to be wound into a ball before use so that the yarn does not become tangled while you are knitting.

Yarn comes in different weights and thicknesses. In some of the patterns lighter wool is used double to create a thicker yarn, and this is noted in the pattern.

Lace weight (1–3-ply) yarn is a very fine yarn that is used for more open patterns. Generally, you get very long yardage in a 50g ball or hank. Sometimes lighter-weight yarns can be doubled to create a more dense look.

Fingering (4-ply) yarn is slightly thinner than light worsted weight yarn (see below) and is popular for knitting shawls and socks.

Light worsted (DK/8-ply) yarn is a medium thickness yarn that is suitable for many projects. The main light worsted (DK/8-ply) yarn used in these projects is made from alpaca wool, with each ball containing 131yd (120m) of yarn.

Worsted (aran/10-ply) yarn is thicker than light worsted (DK/8-ply) yarn and will produce correspondingly thicker items.

Bulky (chunky) or **super bulky** (super chunky) yarn is thicker still and will produce lovely, snuggly items that are ideal for cold weather.

Gauge (tension)

Gauge, or tension, is not as important for scarves and snoods as it is for hats, so I have only given gauge (tension) details where necessary. It is useful to make tension swatches when you are knitting items that need to fit well, such as hats. Each knitter will work slightly more tightly or loosely than the next, so it is just as well to check before you start knitting.

Needles

For most of my projects I use straight needles made from sustainable wood. I find these great to knit with because of their durability, and they are flexible to work with in all temperatures. Unless specified in the patterns, the needles used are single-pointed ones. These come in pairs. I used double-pointed needles in some patterns, which usually come in sets of five.

Some patterns require a circular knitting needle. These are made up of short needle tips of around 10–12.75cm (4–5in) long, joined together by a flexible cord or cable. These needles are great for knitting in the round, but can also be used like ordinary straight needles to knit back and forth rows. They enable you to have long rows of live stitches on the needle.

I used cable needles in some projects; these were also made from sustainable wood and are great to work with, as the yarn does not fall off the needles.

Other equipment

For all of the projects you will need a pair of good-quality, sharp scissors to cut off the ends of your yarn when weaving them into your work.

You may also like to buy a pompom maker for any projects that include pompoms, or you can make them in the traditional way with circles of cardboard.

As well as knitting needles, you will need a blunt-ended needle with a large eye, such as a tapestry needle, for sewing up your projects and weaving in any loose ends.

Stitch markers are used for some patterns. They are used where a specific measurement is required within a pattern.

A crochet hook can also be useful to help make tassels for some of the scarves.

Abbreviations

beg	beginning
C2B	(cross 2 back) slip next st onto cable needle and hold at back of work, knit next st from left-hand needle, then knit st from cable needle
C4B	slip next two sts onto cable needle and hold at back, k2 from left-hand needle, k2 from cable needle
C4F	slip next two sts onto cable needle and hold at front, k2 from left-hand needle, k2 from cable needle
Cr3B	slip next st onto cable needle and hold at back of work, k2, then p1 from cable needle
Cr3F	slip next 2 sts onto a cable needle and hold at front of work, p1, then k2 from cable needle
dec	decrease
DPN	double-pointed needle(s)
g st	garter stitch: knit every row
inc	increase (by working into the front and back of the same stitch)
k	knit
KB1	knit into back of st
knitwise	as though to knit
k2tog	knit 2 stitches together
kfb	knit in front then back of stitch
kfbf	knit into the front, then back, then front of the next st (2 sts increased)
ktbl	knit 1 row through back loop
MB	make bobble
m1	make 1 stitch; pick up the horizontal yarn between the current and the next st, and knit it through back loop
p	purl
patt	work in pattern as established/instructed
pfb	purl in front then back of stitch
PM	place stitch marker
psso	pass slipped stitch over
purlwise	as though to purl
p2tog	purl 2 stitches together
rem	remaining
rep	repeat
RS	right side(s)
sk2po	slip 2 stitches knitwise on to right-hand needle, knit next stitch, then pass the previous slipped stitches over the knitted stitch
sl	slip; usually slip 1 stitch
ssk	slip 2 sts, then knit them together
s2pp	slip 2 sts as if to purl, purl next st, pass 2 slipped sts over
st(s)	stitch(es)
st st	stocking stitch (US stockinette stitch); alternate knit and purl rows (unless directed otherwise, always start with a knit row)
tbl	through back loop
T2B	(twist 2 back) slip next st onto cable needle and hold at back of work, knit next st from left-hand needle, then purl st from cable needle
T3B	(twist 3 back) slip next st onto cable needle and hold at back of work, knit 2, then purl st from cable needle
T2BW	(twist 2 back on wrong side) slip next st onto cable needle and hold at back (right side) of work, knit next st from left-hand needle, then purl st from cable needle

T3F	(twist 3 front) slip next 2 sts onto cable needle and hold at front of work, purl 1 then knit 2 from cable needle
T2FW	(twist 2 front on wrong side) slip next st onto cable needle and hold at front (wrong side) of work, purl next st from left-hand needle, then knit st from cable
WS	wrong side(s)
yfrn	yarn forward and over needle
yfwd	yarn forward
wyrn	wrap yarn around needle to create an extra stitch (this makes up for the stitch you lose when you knit two together)
yo	yarn over
*	repeat the instructions following the * as many times as specified

Fuchsia Scarf

Materials:

» 2 balls of worsted (aran/10-ply) yarn in fuchsia pink; 100g/138yd/126m

Needles:

» 8mm (US 11, UK 0) circular knitting needle

Instructions:

Cast on 178 sts and ktbl to form a neat edge.

SCARF PATTERN

Row 1: *k2, p2*, rep from * to * to end of row.

Rows 2–4: rep row 1 three more times (this pattern is called moss stitch).

Row 5: *k1, wyrn*, rep from * to * to end of row.

Row 6: *k1, drop the wrapped st off the needle*, rep from * to *, knit the last st.

Rows 7 and 8: rep rows 5 and 6.

Rows 9 and 10: knit.

Rows 11–28: rep rows 5–10 three more times.

Rows 29–32: *k2, p2*, rep from * to * to end of row. Cast off.

MAKING UP

Weave in all loose ends.

This is a scarf with a twist as it is knitted using a circular needle as a long needle. The scarf can be knitted to any length simply by adjusting the number of cast-on stitches and the number of rows knitted.

Sparkler Wrist Warmers

SPECIAL STITCH

MB (MAKE BOBBLE): make a bobble all in the same stitch. Knit into front, back and front again of same st, turn. Sl1, k1, psso, k1, pass previous st over. You are now back to the original 1 stitch.

Instructions:

Make two. Using 4mm (US 6, UK 8) needles, cast on 37 sts, then ktbl to form a neat edge.

Next row: k3, *MB, k5*, rep from * to * to last 4 sts, MB, k3.

MAIN PATTERN

Row 1 and every odd-numbered row (WS): purl.

Row 2: *k10, sl1, k1, psso, yfwd*, rep from * to * to last st, k1.

Row 4: k9, sl1, k1, psso, yfwd, *k10, sl1, k1, psso, yfwd*, rep from * to * to last 2 sts, k2.

Row 6: *k8, (sl1, k1, psso, yfwd) twice*, rep from * to * to last st, k1.

Row 8: k7, (sl1, k1, psso, yfwd) twice, *k8, (sl1, k1, psso, yfwd) twice*, rep from * to * to last 2 sts, k2.

Row 10: *k6, (sl1, k1, psso, yfwd) three times*, rep from * to * to last st, k1.

Row 12: k5, (sl1, k1, psso, yfwd) three times, *k6, (sl1, k1, psso, yfwd) three times*, rep from * to * to last 2 sts, k2.

Row 14: *k4, (sl1, k1, psso, yfwd) four times*, rep from * to * to last st, k1.

Row 16: k1, *yfwd, k2tog, k10*, rep from * to * to end of row.

Row 18: k2, yfwd, k2tog, *k10, yfwd, k2tog*, rep from * to * to last 9 sts, k9.

Row 20: k1, *(yfwd, k2tog) twice, k8*, rep from * to * to end of row.

Row 22: k2, (yfwd, k2tog) twice, *k8, (yfwd, k2tog) twice*, rep from * to * to last 7 sts, k7.

Row 24: k1, *(yfwd, k2tog) three times, k6*, rep from * to * to end of row.

Row 26: k2, (yfwd, k2tog) three times, *k6 (yfwd, k2tog) three times*, rep from * to * to last 5 sts, k5.

Row 28: k1, *(yfwd, k2tog) four times, k4*, rep from * to * to end of row.

Rep rows 1–17 once more.

Change to 3.5mm (US 4, UK 9 or 10) needles.

Next row: *k1, p1*, rep from * to * to last st, k1.

Next row: p1, *k1, p1*, rep from * to * to end of row.

Cast off.

MAKING UP

Join the side seams using mattress stitch, 2¾in (7cm) from the wrist end (cast-on edge) and 2in (5cm) from the finger end. This will leave a gap for your thumb to go through. Weave in all loose ends.

These are really pretty beaded cuffs that will brighten up any outfit. The bobbles around the cuff add a little more texture to the fabric.

Lacy Fern Headband

Materials:
» 1 ball of lace weight (1–3-ply) alpaca/silk in fern green;
100g/875yd/800m

Needles:
» 3mm (US 2, UK 11) knitting needles

Instructions:

The lace pattern is knitted in multiples of 8 + 5.

Cast on 37 sts.

Row 1 (RS): knit.

Row 2: purl.

Row 3: k1, p3, *k5, p3, rep from * to last st, k1.

Row 4: p1, k3, *p5, k3, rep from * to last st, p1.

Row 5: k1, yfrn, k3tog, yfrn, *k5, yfrn, k3tog, yfrn, rep from * to last st, k1.

Rows 6–8: st st starting with a purl row.

Row 9: k5, *p3, k5, rep from * to end.

Row 10: p5, *k3, p5, rep from * to end.

Row 11: k5, *yfrn, k3tog, yfrn, k5, rep from * to end.

Row 12: purl.

Repeat these 12 rows until the headband fits snugly around your head with a slight stretch, ending with either a row 6 or a row 12. Cast off.

MAKING UP
With RS of work together, join seams using mattress stitch. Weave in all loose ends.

Twist it, fold it or wear it flat – this headwrap is very versatile. The lacy stitch gives the band movement, so you can create your own look.

Hemingway Boot Cuffs

Materials:
» 2 balls of worsted (aran/10-ply) textured yarn in cream or variegated; 100g/84yd/77m

Needles:
» 5mm (US 8, UK 6) knitting needles
» 6mm (US 10, UK 4) knitting needles
» Cable needle

SPECIAL STITCH

MB (MAKE BOBBLE): to make a bobble, (k1, yo, k1, yo, k1) into next stitch, turn and p5, turn and k1, sl1, k2tog, psso, k1, turn and p3tog. With RS facing, knit into the bobble stitch again.

Instructions:

WOMEN'S SIZE

Make two.

Using 5mm (US 8, UK 6) needles, cast on 52 sts.

Rows 1–21: work rows in k2/p2 rib.

Row 22: using set rib pattern, increase on second and every following twelfth st (56 sts).

MEN'S SIZE

Make two.

Using 5mm (US 8, UK 6) needles, cast on 60 sts.

Rows 1–25: work rows in k2, p2 rib.

Row 26: inc 1 on every fifth st (72 sts).

Change to 6mm (US 10, UK 4) needles and insert knotted cable as follows:

KNOTTED CABLE SECTION

This is worked over 6 sts on a background of reverse st st.

Cable block (RS): k2, p2, k2.

Rows 1, 5, 7 and 9 (women's): p3, *insert cable block, p3* rep from * to * until last 8 sts, insert cable block, p2.

Rows 1, 5, 7 and 9 (men's): p2, *insert cable block, p3* rep from * to * until last 7 sts, insert cable block, p1.

Row 2 and all even rows to row 10 (women's): k2, *p2, k2, p2, k3*, rep from * to * to end of row.

Row 2 and all even rows to row 10: (men's): k1, *insert cable block, k3*, rep from * to * to last 8 sts, insert cable block, k2.

Row 3: p3, *cable 6 – slip next 4 sts on to cable needle and hold at front of work, knit next 2 sts from left-hand needle, then slip the 2 purl sts from the cable needle back to the left-hand needle. Pass the cable needle with 2 rem knit sts to the back of work, purl sts from left-hand needle, then knit the sts from the cable needle; p3*, rep to last 8 sts, repeat cable block once more, p2.

Rows 11–14: as rows 1–4 of set pattern.

BOBBLE ROW

Row 15 (women's): p3, *k2, MB, p1, k2, p3*, rep from * to * until last 8 sts, insert cable block, p2.

Row 15 (men's): p2 *insert cable block, p1, MB, p1*, rep from * to * until last 7 sts, insert cable block, p1.

Remember to knit into the bobble stitch again before continuing with the pattern.

Row 16: as row 2.

Row 17: *k2, p2* rep from * to * until end of row.

Row 18: cast off.

MAKING UP

Weave in all loose ends. With RS facing, use mattress stitch to join the side seams of the pattern component of the boot cuff. Sew up the rib on the rear side of the boot cuff.

Two balls of variegated worsted (aran/10-ply) yarn were used for this version of the boot cuffs. Even a simple change in colour can alter the character of your projects, so have fun experimenting.

Peruvian-style Hat

Materials:
» 1 ball each of worsted (aran/10-ply) yarn in red (A), blue (B) and yellow (C); 50g/103yd/93m

Needles:
» 4.5 mm (US 7, UK 7) knitting needles
» 5mm (US 8, UK 6) knitting needles

Gauge (tension):
» 20 sts x 22 rows = 4in (10cm) square using 5mm (US 8, UK 6) needles over Fair Isle pattern

Instructions:

EAR FLAPS (MAKE TWO IDENTICAL FLAPS)
Using 5mm (US 8, UK 6) needles and yarn A, cast on 3 stitches.
Row 1 (WS): knit.
Row 2 (RS): knit into the front and back of each stitch (6 sts).
Rows 3 and 4: as rows 1 and 2 (12 sts).
Row 5: k4, p4, k4.
Row 6: k4, kfb, k2, kfb, k4 (14 sts).
Row 7: k4, p6, k4.
Row 8: k4, kfb, k4, kfb, k4 (16 sts).
Row 9: k4, p8, k4.
Row 10: knit.
Repeat rows 9 and 10 five more times.
Set aside.

MAIN BODY
Next row (WS): cast on 15 sts using yarn A, work k4, p8, k4 across WS of first ear flap, cast on 38 sts using yarn A, work k4, p8, k4 across WS of second earflap, cast on 15 sts using yarn A (100 sts).
Next row (RS): k15 through the back loop, k16, k38 through the back loop, k16, k15 through the back loop.
Next row: purl.

Now work the 5 rows from chart A, noting that the pattern is repeated six times across the row and then the first 10 sts are repeated once more. Note when working Fair Isle the odd-numbered rows are read from right to left (knit rows) and for even-numbered rows the chart is read from left to right (purl rows). Remember to begin WS row on same st previous RS row ended on.

Chart A

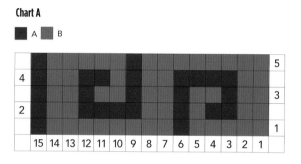

Row 6: using yarn A, purl.
Rows 7 and 8: using yarn A, knit.
Row 9: using yarn C, knit.
Row 10: using yarn C, purl.
Rows 11–21: work from chart B.

Chart B

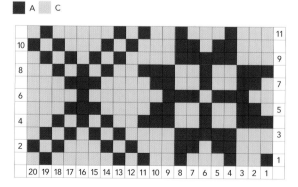

Row 22: using yarn C, purl.

Rows 23 and 24: using yarn C, knit.

Rows 25 and 26: using yarn B, work 2 rows in st st.

Rows 27–33: work from chart C.

Chart C

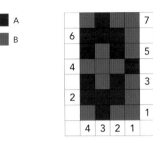

Row 34: using yarn B, purl.

Rows 35 and 36: using yarn B, knit.

Row 37: *k2A, k2C, rep from * to end of row.

Row 38: *p2C, p2A, rep from * to end of row.

Row 39: *k2C, k2A, rep from * to end of row.

Row 40: *p2A, p2C, rep from * to end of row.

Row 41: using yarn B, *k1, sl 1, k1, psso, rep from * to last st, k1 (67 sts).

Row 42: using yarn B, knit.

Row 43: as row 41 (45 sts).

Row 44: using yarn B, purl.

Row 45: *k1, sl 1, k1, psso, rep from * to end of row (30 sts).

Row 46: purl.

Row 47: *k2tog, rep from * to end of row (15 sts).

Thread a needle through sts leaving a long tail end for sewing up.

HAT BORDER

Using yarn A and 4.5mm (US 7, UK 7) needles and with RS of work facing you, pick up and knit 12 sts from straight edge, 28 sts around first ear flap, 30 sts from long straight edge, 28 sts around second ear flap and 12 sts from final straight edge (110 sts).

Cast off.

MAKING UP

Pull yarn up tightly at the top of the hat and fasten off securely. Join back seam using mattress stitch. Weave in all loose ends. Using yarn A, make two plaits approximately 15in (38cm) long and attach to bottom points of ear flaps.

Regal Snood

Materials:
- » 2 balls of light worsted (DK/8-ply) merino wool in two shades of green; 100g/251yd/230m

Tools:
- » 6.5mm (US 10½, UK 3) circular knitting needle
- » 1 stitch marker

Size:
- » Circumference: 26½in (67cm), height: 9½in (24cm)

Tension:
- » 11.5 sts x 25 rows = 4in (10cm) square using 6.5mm (US 10.5, UK 3) needles with yarn doubled

Instructions:

NOTE: the yarn is held double throughout this pattern.

Cast on 77 sts. Place a stitch marker to denote start of each round. Join the round, being careful not to twist any stitches. Slip marker as you pass it on each round.

Round 1: *k1, p1, rep from * to last st, k1.
Round 2: *p1, k1, rep from * to last st, p1.
Repeat these 2 rounds until work measures approximately 9½in (24cm) in height.
Cast off.

MAKING UP
Press snood lightly. Weave in all loose ends.

This simple snood is knitted in moss stitch using a luxurious yarn that blends two colours together. It is knitted in the round and is very quick to make.

Heather & Skye Scarf

Materials:

» 1 ball of super bulky (super chunky) yarn in green/purple variegated; 250g/240½yd/220m
» A large wooden button
» Purple darning yarn

Needles:

» 12mm (US 17, UK 000) knitting needles

KNITTING NOTE

This was made using a handspun and dyed yarn from a cottage industry in Skye, Scotland. I simply knitted the scarf until the yarn ran out. The weight listed is therefore an estimate. Using an easily available bouclé super bulky (super chunky) yarn of approximately 250g and 240½yd (220m) will make a good substitute.

Instructions:

Cast on 9 sts.

SCARF PATTERN

Row 1: k1, *wyrn, k2tog* repeat from * to * to end of row.
Next rows: rep row 1 until work measures 39in (1m).
Cast off.

In this pattern there are significant gaps between some stitches. Instead of making a specific buttonhole, one of these can be used when fastening the button. First, identify such a hole; then, in a position in which it can be fastened comfortably, sew on a button using purple darning yarn.

MAKING UP

Weave in all loose ends.

This scarf was inspired by a visit to Skye. I really loved the colours of the heathers and ferns and so bought handspun and locally dyed wool in colours to match them.

Chic Stripes Wrist Warmers

Materials:

» 2 balls of light worsted (DK/8-ply) merino yarn in light grey (A) and dark grey (B); 100g/273yd/250m
» 2 small, striped buttons

Needles:

» 4mm (US 6, UK 8) knitting needles

Instructions:

RIGHT HAND

Using yarn A, cast on 40 sts, then ktbl to form a neat edge.

Rows 1 and 2: *k2, p2*, rep from * to * to end of row.

Change to yarn B. From this point on, change colours every two rows to form the stripes.

Rows 3–14: st st.

SHAPE FOR THUMB

Row 15: k20, m1, k5, m1, k15 (42 sts).

Rows 16–18: st st, starting with a purl row.

Row 19: k20, m1, k7, m1, k15 (44 sts).

Rows 20–22: st st, starting with a purl row.

Row 23: k20, m1, k9, m1, k15 (46 sts).

Rows 24–26: st st, starting with a purl row.

Row 27: k20, m1, k11, m1, k15 (48 sts).

Rows 28–30: st st, starting with a purl row.

DIVIDE FOR THUMB

Row 31 (RS): k33, turn.

Row 32: p13.

Rows 33–38: working on these 13 sts only, knit in st st, continuing in the stripe sequence.

Row 39: *k2, p2*, rep from * to * to last st, k1.

Row 40: p1, *k2, p2*, rep from * to * to end of row.

Cast off.

Using mattress stitch, sew the side seam of the thumb. With RS facing, rejoin yarn and pick up and knit 2 sts from the base of the thumb, then knit to end of row (37 sts).

Next row: purl.

Next 15 rows: st st.

Next row: *k2, p2*, rep from * to * to last st, k1.

Next row: p1, *k2, p2*, rep from * to * to end of row. Cut off yarn B. Cast off following rib pattern.

LEFT HAND

Work as for right hand up to the shaping for the thumb.

Row 15: k15, m1, k5, m1, k20 (42 sts).

Rows 16–30: work increases as for right hand using the spacing of row 15 above – start increase rows with k15 sts and end with k20 sts.

DIVIDE FOR THUMB

Next row (RS): k28, turn.

Next row: p13.

Next 8 rows: as for right-hand thumb.

Cast off and join the side seam of the thumb. With RS facing, rejoin yarn and pick up and knit 2 sts from base of thumb, then knit to end of row.

Next row: purl.

Next 15 rows: st st.

Next row: *k2, p2*, rep from * to * to last st, k1.

Next row: p1, *k2, p2*, rep from * to * to end of row. Cut off yarn B. Cast off following rib pattern.

BOW (MAKE FOUR)

Cast on 13 sts using 4mm (US 6, UK 8) needles and yarn A, then ktbl to form a neat edge.

Rows 1 and 2: st st.

Cast off. Weave in all loose ends.

MAKING UP

With RS facing, use mattress stitch to sew up the side seams. Match the stripes as you sew up your gloves. Weave in all loose ends.

Place bows on the front of the glove, three light grey stripes down from the finger end. Cross the strips in the centre and place a small, striped button in the middle. Sew the button in place using yarn B (this will also secure the bow onto the glove).

These pretty little gloves will keep your hands warm on a winter's day. I have chosen muted greys for the stripes, but they would be equally pretty in bright or subtle colours.

Lacy Dream Headband

Materials:

» 1 ball of fingering (4-ply) baby alpaca/superfine merino in cobalt blue; 50g/246yd/225m
» Small beads for the borders

Needles:

» 3.25mm (US 3, UK 10) knitting needles

KNITTING NOTE

Cut off six long lengths of yarn prior to casting on, to work the beads in. While knitting your pattern, use a long end of yarn at either side of the headband and knit it as you go along – this makes it easy to thread in your beads using a narrow-eyed needle. I found it helpful to knit the first and last stitch of alternate rows with both the yarn from the main pattern and the end yarn, to avoid loops forming up the side of the work.

Instructions:

Cast on 3 sts. Sew in one bead at the point of your work.
Row 1: knit.
Row 2: k1, inc1, k1, inc1, k1 (5 sts).
Row 3: knit.
Row 4: k2, inc1, knit to last st, inc1, k1 (7 sts).
Repeat the last 2 rows until there are 29 sts, inserting a bead at either side of the work on row 12.
Next row: knit.
Next row: k2, inc1, knit to end of row (30 sts).
Continue in the following lace pattern, inserting one bead at each end on every first row of pattern sequence.
Rows 1–4: knit.
Row 5: k2, *sl1, k1, psso, k4, yfrn, k1, yfrn, k4, k2tog, rep from * to last 2 sts, k2.
Rows 6, 8, 10 and 12: purl.

Row 7: k2, *sl1, k1, psso, (k3, yfrn) twice, k3, k2tog, rep from * to last 2 sts, k2.
Row 9: k2, *sl1, k1, psso, k2, yfrn, k2tog, yfrn, k1, yfrn, sl1, k1, psso, yfrn, k2, k2tog, rep from * to last 2 sts, k2.
Row 11: k2, *sl1, k1, psso, k1, yfrn, k2tog, yfrn, k3, yfrn, sl1, k1, psso, yfrn, k1, k2tog, rep from * to last 2 sts, k2.
Row 13: k2, *sl1, k1, psso, (yfrn, k2tog) twice, yfrn, k1, (yfrn, sl1, k1, psso) twice, yfrn, k2tog, rep from * to last 2 sts, k2.
Row 14: purl.
Continue the 14-row pattern repeat until the headband fits snugly around your head, ending with row 4 of the pattern.
Cast off.

MAKING UP

Block work carefully. With RS facing, place the shaped end (cast-on end) over the cast-off edge and sew in place. Turn the work over and sew the seam at the back to secure it. Weave in all loose ends.

Bramble Boot Cuffs

Materials:
» 3 balls of super bulky (super chunky) yarn in purple; 100g/87½yd/80m

Tools:
» 7mm (US 10½, UK 2) DPN, 7½in (19cm) long
» 10mm (US 15, UK 000) circular knitting needle, 23½in (60cm) long
» Stitch marker

Instructions:

CUFFS
Make two.

Using 7mm (US 10½, UK 2) DPN, cast on 29 sts, distributing the stitches evenly across the four needles.

Do not turn work. Join this first round by slipping the first cast-on stitch on to the left-hand needle. PM on right-hand needle (this is to mark the beginning of the round), and knit this slipped stitch together with the last cast-on stitch. You will now have 28 sts (7 on each of the DPNs).

Rows 1–16: *k1, p 1* rep to end of row. These 16 rows form the cuff of the piece. Be careful to move your stitch marker at the end of each row.

LEGS
Continuing from the cuffs, change to the 10mm (US 15, UK 000) circular needle and begin bramble stitch as follows. The pattern repeat is over 4 rounds. Remember to PM after each completed round.

Round 1: purl.

Round 2: *p1, k1, p1* all into next st, k3 together, rep set pattern to the end of round.

Round 3: purl.

Round 4: k3tog, *p1, k1, p1*, rep set pattern to end of round.

These 4 rounds create the bramble stitch. Rep the 4 rounds once more and then rep row 1 once more. Cast off purlwise.

MAKING UP
Weave in all loose ends.

These boot cuffs will give a different look to a favourite pair of boots. Try knitting them in cream yarn for a classic monochrome look.

Green Patterned Cap

Materials:
» 1 ball each of light worsted (DK/8-ply) yarn in light green (A), rust (B), dark grey (C), mauve (D) and yellow (E); 50g/191yd/175m

Needles:
» 4mm (US 6, UK 8) knitting needles

Gauge (tension):
» 19 sts x 28 rows = 4in (10cm) square using 4mm (US 6, UK 8) needles over Fair Isle pattern

Instructions:

MAIN BODY
Using yarn C, cast on 124 sts.
Rows 1–9: *k2, p2, rep from * to end.
Next 2 rows: knit (these rows will form fold line).
Start working from the chart below:

Chart

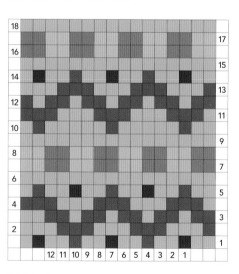

A B C D E

Work 2 edge stitches, then repeat 12-stitch pattern ten times, followed by the 2 remaining edge stitches, noting that all odd-numbered rows are knitted reading chart from right to left, and all even-numbered rows are purled reading chart from left to right. Remember to twist the yarn each time you change colour. Work the 18-row pattern from the chart twice to form the body of the hat. Cast off.

TOP
When working the top, work first row in yarn A, then alternate between yarns B and A, working in 6-row stripes and finishing with yarn A on last row.
Cast on 16 sts using yarn A.
Row 1: kfb, k to last st, kfb (18 sts).
Row 2: pfb three times, p to last 3 sts, pfb three times (24 sts).
Row 3: kfb, k to last st, kfb (26 sts).
Row 4: pfb twice, p to last 2 sts, pfb twice (30 sts).
Row 5: kfb, k to last st, kfb (32 sts).
Row 6: pfb, k to last st, pfb (34 sts).
Row 7: kfb, k to last st, kfb (36 sts).
Row 8: purl.
Row 9: kfb, k to last st, kfb (38 sts).
Row 10: purl.
Rows 11 and 12: as rows 5 and 6 (42 sts).
Rows 13–32: work in st st for 10 rows.
Row 33: ssk (slip 1 st knitwise, slip next st knitwise, insert left needle into front of both sts, knit together through back loop), k to last 2 sts, k2tog (40 sts).
Row 34: purl.
Rows 35 and 36: as rows 33 and 34 (38 sts).
Row 37: ssk, k to last 2 sts, k2tog (36 sts).
Row 38: p2tog, p to last 2 sts, p2tog (34 sts).
Rows 39 and 40: as rows 37 and 38 (30 sts).
Row 41: ssk twice, k to last 4 sts, k2tog twice (26 sts).
Row 42: p2tog, p to last 2 sts, p2tog (24 sts).
Row 43: ssk three times, k to last 6 sts, k2tog three times (18 sts).
Row 44: p2tog, p to last 2 sts, p2tog (16 sts).
Cast off.

MAKING UP

With RS facing, join the top of the brim to the top of the hat, easing your work as you sew. Using mattress stitch and RS facing, join the side seams. Turn the ribbing to the WS of the hat and sew into place using slip stitch. Weave in all loose ends.

Summer Garden Snood

Materials:
» 2 balls of fingering (4-ply) merino/silk yarn in variegated blue-lilac; 100g/437yd/400m
» 4 buttons of choice

Needles:
» 3.5mm (US 4, UK 9 or 10) knitting needles

Size:
» Circumference: 49½in (126cm), width: 9in (23cm)

Gauge (tension):
» 34 sts x 27 rows = 4in (10cm) square using 3.5mm (US 4, UK 9 or 10) needles over pattern

Instructions:

Cast on 78 sts and ktbl to form a neat edge.

Row 1 (RS): k3, *sl 1, k2tog, psso, k7, yfwd, k1, yfrn, p2, yon, k1, yfwd, k7, k3tog, rep from * twice more, k3.

Row 2 and every even row: k3, *p11, k2, p11, rep from * twice more, k3.

Row 3: k3, *sl 1, k2tog, psso, k6, (yfwd, k1) twice, p2, (k1, yfwd) twice, k6, k3tog, rep from * twice more, k3.

Row 5: k3, *sl 1, k2tog, psso, k5, yfwd, k1, yfwd, k2, p2, k2, yfwd, k1, yfwd, k5, k3tog, rep from * twice more, k3.

Row 7: k3, *sl 1, k2tog, psso, k4, yfwd, k1, yfwd, k3, p2, k3, yfwd, k1, yfwd, k4, k3tog, rep from * twice more, k3.

Row 9: k3, *s1, k2tog, psso, k3, yfwd, k1, yfwd, k4, p2, k4, yfwd, k1, yfwd, k3, k3tog, rep from * twice more, k3.

Row 10: as row 2.

Repeat this 10-row pattern until work measures approximately 49½in (126cm) ending with a row 10.

Cast off, leaving a long yarn tail for sewing up your work.

MAKING UP

Press snood lightly. Sew on buttons in the centre of the four scallops. Overlap the scalloped edges on the back of the snood and sew into place. Weave in all loose ends.

This spring or summer snood is knitted in a lace pattern that highlights the variegated colour of the yarn. The snood is worn by wrapping it twice round your neck.

College Stripe Scarf

Materials:

» 4 balls of light worsted (DK/8-ply) yarn: 3 in grey (A) and 1 in rust (B); 50g/144yd/132m

Needles:

» 5mm (US 8, UK 6) knitting needles

Instructions:

Use the yarns doubled throughout the pattern.

Using yarn A, cast on 220 sts.

Rows 1–3: *k2, p2*, repeat from * to * until end of the row. Change to yarn B.

Row 4: knit.

Row 5: purl.

Rows 6 and 7: rep rows 4 and 5, cut off yarn B.

Rows 8–29: using yarn A, work st st. Change to yarn B.

Rows 30–33: work st st, cut off yarn B.

Row 34: knit one row using yarn A.

Rows 35–37: rep rows 1–3.

Cast off.

MAKING UP

Weave in all loose ends.

This is a really easy scarf that I knitted using straight needles, but it could equally be knitted using circular needles by using them in the same way as you would straight ones. The pattern was inspired by the classic college stripe, although I have only used two colours. You could do this using many colours to form vertical stripes once the stitches are cast off.

Lilac Wrist Warmers

Materials:
» 1 ball of fingering (4-ply) yarn in variegated purple; 100g/328yd/300m
» 39in (1m) narrow purple ribbon

Needles:
» 4mm (US 6, UK 8) knitting needles
» 3.25mm (US 3, UK 10) knitting needles
» 1 cable needle

Instructions:

BELL BORDER
Make two. Using 3.25mm (US 3, UK 10) needles, cast on 52 sts, then ktbl to form a neat edge.

Row 1 (RS): *p2, (k1, p1) four times, k1, p2*, rep from * to * to end of row.

Row 2: *k2, (p1, k1) four times, p1, k2*, rep from * to * to end of row.

Rows 3 and 4: rep rows 1 and 2.

Row 5: *p2, k1, p1, ssk, k1, k2tog, p1, k1, p2*, rep from * to * to end of row (44 sts).

Row 6: *k2, p1, k1, p3, k1, p1, k2*, rep from * to * to end of row.

Row 7: *p2, k1, p1, sl2 knitwise, k1, pass the two slipped sts over one at a time, p1, k1, p2*, rep from * to * to end of row (36 sts).

Row 8: *k2, (p1, k1) twice, p1, k2*, rep from * to * to end of row.

Row 9: *p2, ssk, k1, k2tog, p2*, rep from * to * to end of row (28 sts).

Row 10: *k2, p3, k2*, rep from * to * to end of row.

Row 11: *p2, sl next three sts onto a cable needle, wrap yarn around the stitches twice, then knit the stitches from the cable needle, p2*, rep from * to * to end of row.

Row 12: *k2, p3, k2*, rep from * to * to end of row.

Change to 4mm (US 6, UK 8) needles.

Row 13: *k4, inc1, k1, inc1*, rep from * to * to last 3 sts, knit to end of row (38 sts).

Row 14: purl.

MAIN PATTERN
Row 1: k2 *yfwd, k2tog* rep from * to * to last 2 sts, k2.

Row 2: purl.

Continue working in st st until work measures 7¼in (18.5cm).

Change to 3.25mm (US 3, UK 10) needles.

Now rep rows 1 and 2 of main pattern.

Next row: k2tog, p1, *k1, p1*, rep from * to * to last 3 sts, k2tog, p1 (36 sts).

Next row: *k1, p1*, rep from * to * to end of row.

Cast off.

MAKING UP
With RS facing, join the side seams using mattress stitch, 2¾in (7cm) from the wrist end, starting after the bell border (the bell border will be left open) and 2³/₈in (6cm) from the finger end. This will leave a gap for your thumb to go through. Weave in all loose ends. Thread the ribbon through every other gap on the finger end, starting the threading at the centre front. Tie the ribbon together with a bow.

These feminine wrist warmers are made in a fine mohair with a pretty border and ribbon edging.

Snowflake Headband

Instructions:

Using yarn A, cast on 108 sts, then ktbl to form a neat edge.

Rows 1 and 2: *k1, p1, rep from * to end of row.

Row 3: *k3B, k1A, rep from * to end of row.

Row 4: p2B, *p1A, p3B, rep from * to last 2 sts, p1A, p1B.

Row 5: using yarn A, knit.

Row 6: using yarn A, purl.

Row 7: work chart row 1 eight times across row in knit, k4A.

Continue working from the chart; odd-numbered rows are knitted working from right to left, and even-numbered rows are purled working from left to right.

Next row: using yarn A, purl.

Next row: using yarn A, knit.

Next row: *p1A, p3B, rep from * to end of row.

Next row: k1B, *k1A, k3B, rep from * to last 3 sts, k1A, k2B.

Cut off yarn B.

Next row: purl.

Next row: knit.

Work next 2 rows as rows 1 and 2 of pattern.

Cast off.

MAKING UP

With RS facing, join seams together using mattress stitch. Weave in all loose ends.

13	12	11	10	9	8	7	6	5	4	3	2	1	

Chart rows numbered 1–11.

This headband will complement any winter outfit in these soft, neutral colours.

Penguin Boot Cuffs

Materials:

» 5 balls of light worsted (DK/8-ply) pure alpaca yarn: 2 in pale turquoise (A) and 1 each in gold (B), mid-blue (C) and cream (D); 50g/109yd/100m

Needles:

» 5mm (US 8, UK 6) knitting needles

Instructions:

Make two.

Using yarn A, cast on 58 sts and ktbl to form a neat edge.

Using the chart place pattern as follows:

Even row numbers are knit and odd numbers are purl.

Row 1: k2A, *3B, 2A, 3B, 6A* rep from * to * three more times.

Continue working from the chart until row 18. Cut off yarn C. The rest of the knitting is done in yarn A.

Row 19: knit.

Row 20: purl.

Now continue in ribbing.

RIBBING

Row 1: *k2, p2* rep until the last two sts, k2.

Row 2: *p2, k2* rep until the last two sts, p2.

Rows 3–20: rep rows 1 and 2 nine more times.

Row 21: as row 1.

Row 22: cast off.

MAKING UP

Weave in all loose ends. With RS facing, use mattress stitch to join the side seams of the pattern component of the boot cuff. Sew up the rib on the rear side of the boot cuff.

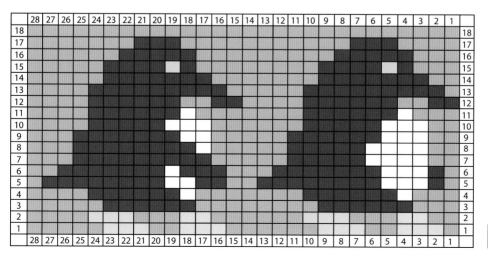

	A	B	C	D

38

Penguins are always fun to work with and these cuffs will liven up any boots. This pattern is suitable for a knitter who has mastered the basics. To change the look, try knitting them in different colours.

Winter Walkies Hat

Materials:

» 2 balls of worsted (aran/10-ply) alpaca/merino blend in blue (A), a small amount in red (B) and 1 ball in beige (C); 50g/94m/103yd

Needles:

» 4.5mm (US 7, UK 7) knitting needles
» 5mm (US 8, UK 6) knitting needles

Gauge (tension):

» 20 sts x 22 rows = 4in (10cm) square using 5mm (US 8, UK 6) needles over pattern

Instructions:

Using 4.5mm (US 7, UK 7) needles and yarn A, cast on 102 sts, then ktbl to form a neat edge.

Rows 1–26: *k1, p1, rep from * to end of row.

Change to 5mm (US 8, UK 6) needles.

Rows 27 and 28: using yarn A, work 2 rows in st st.

Chart A

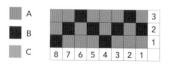

NOTE: When working Fair Isle the odd-numbered rows are read from right to left (knit rows) and for even-numbered rows the chart is read from left to right (purl rows).

Rows 29–31: work from chart A, repeating the pattern twelve times and then the first 6 sts once. On the second row the pattern starts on stitch 6, working back to stitch 1, then repeat the full pattern to end.

Row 32: using yarn A, purl.

Rows 33–48: work from chart B, setting spacing as follows: k1A *work sts 1–19 from chart, k1A, rep from * to last st, k1A.

Rows 49 and 50: using yarn A, work 2 rows in st st.

Chart B

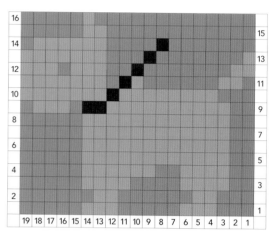

Rows 51–53: as rows 29–31.

Rows 54–56: work in st st starting with a purl row.
Cut off yarn A.

SHAPING THE CROWN

Row 57: using yarn B *k2tog, rep from * to end of row (51 sts).

Row 58: purl.

Row 59: k1, *k2tog, rep from * to end of row (26 sts).

Row 60: purl.

MAKING UP

Cut yarn and thread through remaining stitches. Pull yarn up tightly and fasten off securely. Join back seam using mattress stitch. Weave in all loose ends.

Foxy Boxy Snood

Materials:
» 4 balls of light worsted (DK/8-ply) superfine alpaca yarn in cream;
50g/131yd/120m

Needles:
» 8mm (US 11, UK 0) knitting needles

Size:
» Circumference: 32¼in (82cm), height 15¾in (40cm)

Gauge (tension):
» 11 sts x 16 rows = 4in (10cm) square using 8mm (US 11, UK 0)
needles over pattern

Instructions:

NOTE: The yarn is used double throughout.

Cast on 45 sts then ktbl to form a neat edge.

Row 1 (RS): knit.

Row 2: purl.

Row 3: k1, p3, *k5, p3, rep from * to last st, k1.

Row 4: p1, k3, *p5, k3, rep from * to last st, p1.

Row 5: k1, *yfwd, k3tog, yfwd, k5, rep from * to last 4 sts, yfwd,
k3tog, yfwd, k1.

Rows 6–8: work in st st, starting with a purl row.

Row 9: k5, *p3, k5, rep from * to end.

Row 10: p5, *k3, p5, rep from * to end.

Row 11: k5, *yfwd, k3tog, yfwd, k5, rep from * to end.

Row 12: purl.

Rep these 12 rows until work measures approximately 32¼in
(82cm).

Cast off, leaving a long yarn tail for sewing up your work.

MAKING UP
Press snood lightly. Join cast-on and cast-off ends using mattress
stitch with RS facing. Weave in all loose ends.

This is a very snuggly snood made
from a gorgeous alpaca yarn that
is really soft. Holding the yarn
double gives it a really chunky feel
and the simple lace pattern adds
texture and interest.

Frivolous Florence Scarf

Materials:
» 2 balls of lace weight (1–3-ply) yarn in variegated purple/green; 50g/437yd/400m
» 59in (150cm) length of ribbon for edging

Needles:
» 4mm (US 6, UK 8) knitting needles

Instructions:
Cast on 52 sts.

SCARF PATTERN

Row 1: knit.
Row 2: purl.
Row 3: k4, *yo, sl1, k1, psso, k2tog, yo, k4*, repeat from * to *.
Row 4: purl.
Next rows: rep rows 1–4 pattern until work measures 74¾in (190cm).
Cast off.

MAKING UP

Weave in all loose ends. Weave the ribbon into the holes like a running stitch. Turn back the edge and, using your knitting yarn, make a neat hem at either side of the ribbon. Press the scarf lightly.

This scarf was inspired by a visit to Tuscany. I knitted it in a variegated lace yarn and then threaded some ribbons in at the ends to add a bit of chic. Wrap it around your neck once or twice, depending on the look you want.

Fair Isle Wrist Warmers

Materials:

» 1 ball each of light worsted (DK/8-ply) alpaca yarn in midnight blue (A), mustard (B) and cream (C); 50g/131yd/120m

Needles:

» 4mm (US 6, UK 8) knitting needles

Instructions:

Make two. Using yarn A, cast on 40 sts, then ktbl to form a neat edge.

Rows 1 and 2: *k1, p1*, rep from * to * to end of row.

Row 3: using yarn B, knit, inc 4 sts evenly across the row (44 sts).

Note that you are increasing only on row 3.

Row 4: using yarn B, purl.

Rows 5 and 7: k1B, *k1A, k3B*, rep from * to * to last 3 sts, k1A, k2B.

Row 6: *p1B, p1A*, rep from * to * to end of row.

Rows 8 and 9: starting with a purl row and using yarn B, st st.

Rows 10 and 12: *p1A, p3B*, rep from * to * to end of row.

Row 11: *k1A, k1B*, rep from * to * to end of row.

Rows 13 and 14: using yarn B, st st.

Rows 15 and 16: using yarn A, knit. Cut off yarn A.

Rows 17 and 18: using yarn C, knit.

Rows 19–30: work as rows 3–14, substituting yarn C for yarn A.

Rows 31 and 32: using yarn C, knit.

Rows 33 and 34: using yarn A, knit.

Rows 35–46: as rows 3–14. Cut off yarn B.

Row 47: using yarn A, knit.

Row 48: cast off.

MAKING UP

Join side seams using mattress stitch, 2¾in (7cm) from the wrist end (cast-on edge) and 2in (5cm) from the finger end. This will leave a gap for your thumb to go through. Weave in all loose ends.

These cuffs are decorated with a classic Fair Isle pattern. I have chosen contemporary colours but these could be adapted to suit your taste.

Gooseberry Headband

Materials:
» 1 ball of light worsted (DK/8-ply) merino/alpaca yarn in gooseberry; 50g/124yd/113m
» 2 buttons

Needles:
» 4mm (US 6, UK 8) knitting needles

Instructions:
Cast on 9 sts and ktbl in every st.

Row 1 (buttonhole row): k4, cast off 2 sts, knit to end.

Row 2: k3, cast on 2 sts using cable cast on method, k4.

Row 3: inc1, knit to last st, inc1 (11 sts).

Row 4: p1, *yrn, p2tog, rep from * to end of row.

Rep rows 3 and 4 until there are 17 sts.

LACE PATTERN

Row 1 (RS): sl1, yfrn, k3, sl1, k1, psso, p5, k2tog, k3, yfrn, k1.

Row 2: sl1, p5, k5, p6.

Row 3: sl1, k1, yfrn, k3, sl1, k1, psso, p3, k2tog, k3, yfrn, k2.

Row 4: sl1, p6, k3, p7.

Row 5: sl1, k2, yfrn, k3, sl1, k1, psso, p1, k2tog, k3, yfrn, k3.

Row 6: sl1, p7, k1, p8.

Row 7: sl1, k3, yfrn, k3, sl1, k2tog, psso, k3, yfrn, k4.

Row 8: sl1, purl to last st.

Rep the last 8 rows until work measures 46cm (18in) or desired length, and is long enough to go around your head with a slight stretch (ending on a row 8).

Row 1: k1, k2tog, knit to last 3 sts, k2tog, k1 (15 sts).

Row 2: p1, *yfrn, p2tog, rep from * to end of row.

Rep the last 2 rows until there are 9 sts.

Next row: knit.

Cast off.

MAKING UP

Sew a button on the cast-off end to correspond with the buttonhole on the cast-on end. Sew another button in the centre of the front (optional). Weave in all loose ends.

This neat, decorative headband is great for all ages. Simply knit it to the length required (it should fit snugly around the head with a bit of stretch) and add a pretty button as a detail.

Quackers Boot Cuffs

Materials:

» I ball each of light worsted (DK/8-ply) pure alpaca yarn in teal (A), turquoise (B), gold (C) and red (D); 50g/109yd/100m

Needles:

» 5mm (US 8, UK 6) knitting needles
» 4.5mm (US 7, UK 7) knitting needles

KNITTING NOTE

Twist the yarn every three to four sts to avoid long loops forming at the back of your work.

Instructions:

Make two.

Using 5mm (US 8, UK 6) needles and yarn A, cast on 50 sts then ktbl to form a neat edge. Change to 4.5mm (US 7, UK 7) needles.

Rows 1–15: *k1, p1*. Cut off yarn A.

PATTERN

Row 1: using yarn B, knit row, increasing 1 st in the middle (51 sts).

Row 2: purl.

Rows 3–13: follow chart, working from right to left and with the chart upside down (this is so the ducks are facing the right way when the boot cuff is completed).

Place motif on first row as follows: k4B, k4C, k9B, k4C, k9B, k4C, k9B, k4C, k4B. This is the set format for the pattern as the complete grid is repeated twice across the width of the boot cuff. All odd-numbered rows are knit and even-numbered rows are purl. Cut off yarn C.

Rows 14–16: st st.

Row 17: cast off using picot cast-off as follows: cast off 2 sts, *slip remaining st on right-hand needle onto left-hand needle, cast on 2 sts using cable method, cast off 4 sts*. Rep from * to * to end of row. Fasten off last stitch.

MAKING UP

Weave in all loose ends. With RS facing, use mattress stitch to join the side seams of the pattern component of the boot cuff. Sew up the rib on the rear side of the boot cuff.

	23	22	21	20	19	18	17	16	15	14	13	12	11	10	9	8	7	6	5	4	3	2	1	
12																								12
11																								11
10									█					█										10
9									█	█				█	█									9
8																								8
7																								7
6																								6
5																								5
4																								4
3																								3
2																								2
1																								1
	23	22	21	20	19	18	17	16	15	14	13	12	11	10	9	8	7	6	5	4	3	2	1	

B	C	D
		█

Lovely weather for ducks! These boot cuffs look great and add character to children's Wellingtons or other boots. This pattern is suitable for a knitter who has mastered the basics.

Fair Isle Tam

Materials:
- » 1 ball each of light worsted (DK/8-ply) alpaca yarn in sandstone (A), damson (B), rose (C) and parchment (D); 50g/123yd/112m

Needles:
- » 3.75mm (US 5, UK 9) knitting needles
- » 4mm (US 6, UK 8) knitting needles
- » 1 cable needle

Gauge (tension):
- » 28 sts x 28 rows = 4in (10cm) square using 4mm (US 6, UK 8) needles over Fair Isle pattern

A   B   C   D

Chart A

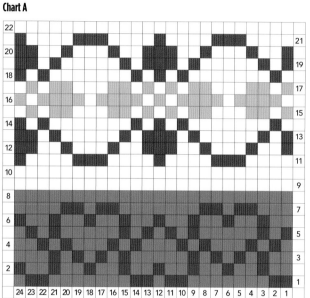

Chart B (decreasing for crown)

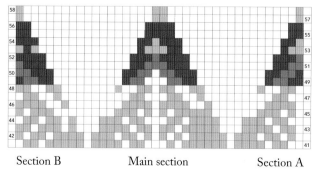

Section B   Main section   Section A

Instructions:

Please check gauge (tension) carefully before starting.

Using 3.75mm (US 5, UK 9) needles and yarn A, cast on 112 sts.

Row 1 (RS): *k2, C4F, rep from * to last 4 sts, k4.

Row 2: purl.

Row 3: knit.

Row 4: purl.

Rows 5 and 6: as rows 1 and 2.

Row 7: *C4B, k2 rep from * to end of row.

Row 8: purl.

Rows 9 and 10: as rows 3 and 4.

Rows 11 and 12: as rows 7 and 8.

Row 13: k1, *M1, k2, rep from * to last st, M1, k1 (168 sts).

Row 14: purl.

Change to 4mm (US 6, UK 8) needles.

Cut off yarn A.

Now work with yarn B (main) and yarn C.

Start working from row 1 of chart A, noting the odd-numbered rows are knitted and worked from right to left and the even-numbered rows are purled and worked from left to right. Continue working from chart until row 22.

Rows 23 and 24: using yarn B, st st.

Rows 25–32: as rows 1–8 of chart A.

DECREASING FOR CROWN

Row 33: using yarn A, *k10, k2tog tbl, k2tog, k10, rep from * seven times (154 sts).

Row 34: purl (154 sts).

When decreasing for the crown in the following rows, follow chart B and work RS (odd-numbered) rows by working section A once, then decreasing as instructed using appropriate colour, then working repeats of the main body followed by decreases as written on instruction rows and finally working section B.

When working the WS (even-numbered) rows, work section B once, purl 2 using appropriate colour, followed by repeats of the main body stitches as written on instruction rows, working final stitches from section A.

Row 35: *patt 9 sts, k2tog tbl, k2tog, patt 9 sts, rep from * seven times (140 sts).

Row 36: *patt 9 sts, p2, patt 9 sts, rep from * seven times.

Row 37: *patt 8 sts, k2tog tbl, k2tog, patt 8 sts, rep from * seven times (126 sts).

Row 38: *patt 8 sts, p2, patt 8 sts, rep from * seven times.

Row 39: *patt 7 sts, k2tog tbl, k2tog, patt 7 sts, rep from * seven times (112 sts).

Row 40: *patt 7 sts, p2, patt 7 sts, rep from * seven times.

Row 41: *patt 6 sts, k2tog tbl, k2tog, patt 6 sts, rep from * seven times (98 sts).

Row 42: *patt 6 sts, p2, patt 6 sts, rep from * 7 times.

Row 43: *patt 5 sts, k2tog tbl, k2tog, patt 5 sts, rep from * seven times (84 sts).

Row 44: *patt 5 sts, p2, patt 5 sts, rep from * seven times.

Row 45: *patt 4 sts, k2tog tbl, k2tog, patt 4, rep from * seven times (70 sts).

Row 46: *patt 4 sts, p2, patt 4 sts, rep from * seven times.

Row 47: *patt 3 sts, k2tog tbl, k2tog, patt 3 sts, rep from * seven times (56 sts).

Row 48: *patt 3 sts, p2, patt 3 sts, rep from * seven times.

Row 49: *patt 2 sts, k2tog tbl, k2tog, patt 2 sts, rep from * seven times (42 sts).

Row 50: *patt 2 sts, p2, patt 2 sts, rep from * seven times.

Row 51: *patt 1 st, k2tog tbl, k2tog, patt 1 st, rep from * seven times (28 sts).

Row 52: *patt 1 st, p2, patt 1 st, rep from * seven times.

Row 53: using yarn A, *k2tog tbl, k2tog, rep from * to end (14 sts).

Row 54: *p2tog, rep from * to end of row (7 sts).

Cut yarn and thread through remaining stitches. Pull up yarn tightly and fasten off securely.

MAKING UP

Sew up side seams using mattress stitch. Weave in all loose ends. Make a short i-cord in yarn A and sew it onto the top of your tam.

Leaf Scarf

Materials:

» 3 balls of worsted (aran/10-ply) baby alpaca/merino yarn in beige; 50g/103yd/94m

Needles:

» 5.5mm (US 9, UK 5) knitting needles

» 1 cable needle

Size:

» Circumference: 46in (117cm), height: 7½in (19cm)

Gauge (tension):

» 19 sts x 23 rows = 4in (10cm) square using 5.5mm (US 9, UK 5) needles over pattern

Instructions:

Cast on 44 sts and ktbl to form a neat edge.

NOTE: in order to stop the edges curling, each odd-numbered row starts with p1, k1, p1, k1 and ends with k1, p1, k1, p1. The even-numbered rows start with k1, p1, k1, p1 and end with p1, k1, p1, k1. These sts are not included in the following instructions.

Pattern is knitted over 32 rows and repeated four times across the row.

Row 1 (RS): C2F, p7.
Row 2: k6, T2FW, p1.
Row 3: KB1, p1, C2F, p5.
Row 4: k4, T2FW, p1, k1, p1.
Row 5: (KB1, p1) twice, C2F, p3.
Row 6: k2, T2FW, (p1, k1) twice, p1.
Row 7: (KB1, p1) three times, C2F, p1.
Row 8: T2FW, (p1, k1) three times, p1.
Row 9: (KB1, p1) four times, KB1.
Row 10: (p1, k1) three times, p1, T2FW.
Row 11: p1, T2F, (p1, KB1) three times.
Row 12: (p1, k1) twice, p1, T2FW, k2.
Row 13: p3, T2F, (p1, KB1) twice.
Row 14: p1, k1, p1, T2FW, k4.
Row 15: p5, T2F, p1, KB1.
Row 16: p1, T2FW, k6.
Row 17: p7, C2B.
Row 18: p1, T2BW, k6.
Row 19: p5, C2B, p1, KB1.
Row 20: p1, k1, p1, T2BW, k4.
Row 21: p3, C2B, (p1, KB1) twice.
Row 22: (p1, k1) twice, p1, T2BW, k2.
Row 23: p1, C2B, (p1, KB1) three times.

Row 24: (p1, k1) three times, p1, T2BW.
Row 25: (KB1, p1) four times, KB1.
Row 26: T2BW, (p1, k1) three times, p1.
Row 27: (KB1, p1) three times, T2B, p1.
Row 28: k2, T2BW, (p1, k1) twice, p1.
Row 29: (KB1, p1) twice, T2B, p3.
Row 30: k4, T2BW, p1, k1, p1.
Row 31: KB1, p1, T2B, p5.
Row 32: k6, T2BW, p1.

Rep these 32 rows until work measures approximately 46in (117cm). Cast off, leaving a long yarn tail for sewing up your work.

MAKING UP

Press snood lightly. Join cast-on and cast-off ends using mattress stitch with RS facing. Weave in all loose ends.

This snood is made using a non-traditional cable. I have used a classic colour that will go with most things.

Parisienne Chic Scarf

Materials:

» 2 balls of lace weight (1–3-ply) yarn in light pink;
  50g/437yd/400m

Needles:

» 4mm (US 6, UK 8) knitting needles

Instructions:

Cast on 56 sts, then ktbl to form a neat edge.

SCARF PATTERN

Rows 1–4: knit.

Row 5: *k1, wyrn*, repeat from * to * until last stitch, k1.

Row 6: *k1, drop the stitch you wrapped in previous row*, repeat from * to * until last stitch, k1.

Rep rows 1–6 until you have knitted 72½in (184cm), finishing with 4 rows of garter stitch.

Cast off.

MAKING UP

Weave in all loose ends.

This is a simple scarf that has been knitted in a very fine lace yarn. You can drape it in many ways and it is a great asset to a spring or summer wardrobe.

Cable Wrist Warmers

Materials:
» 2 balls of light worsted (DK/8-ply) yarn in fawn; 50g/131yd/120m

Needles:
» 4mm (US 6, UK 8) knitting needles
» 4.5mm (US 7, UK 7) knitting needles
» 1 cable needle

SPECIAL STITCHES
CR3F: slip next 2 sts onto a cable needle and hold at front of work, p1, then k2 from cable needle.

CR3B: slip next st onto cable needle and hold at back of work, k2, then p1 from cable needle.

C4B: place 2 sts on to a cable needle and place at back of work. Knit next 2 sts, then knit 2 sts from cable needle.

C4F: place 2 sts on to a cable needle and place at front of work. Knit next 2 sts, then knit 2 sts from cable needle.

Instructions:
The pattern is the same for both hands, and the yarn is used double throughout.

Using 4mm (US 6, UK 8) needles cast on 37 sts, then ktbl to form a neat edge.

Row 1: *k1, p1*, rep from * to * last st, k1.

Row 2: *p1, k1*, rep from * to * last st, p1.

Rows 3–16: as rows 1 and 2, except inc 1 st at the start and inc 1 st at the end of row 16 (39 sts).

Change to 4.5mm (US 7, UK 7) needles for the following cable section of the pattern.

Rows 1, 3, 9 and 11 (WS): *p2, k2, p2, k1, p2, k2, p2*, rep from * to * twice more.

Row 2: *k2, p2, slip next 3 sts onto cable needle and hold at back of work, k2, slip the purl st from cable needle back onto left-hand needle and purl it, k2 from cable needle, p2, k2*, rep from * to * twice more.

Rows 4 and 12: *CR3F, CR3B, p1, CR3F, CR3B*, rep from * to * twice more.

Rows 5, 7, 13 and 15: *k1, p4, k3, p4, k1*, rep from * to * twice more.

Rows 6 and 14: *p1, C4B, p3, C4F, p1*, rep from * to * twice more.

Rows 8 and 16: *CR3B, CR3F, p1, CR3B, CR3F*, rep from * to * twice more.

Row 10: *k2, p2, slip next 3 sts onto cable needle and hold at front of work, k2, slip the purl st from cable needle back onto left-hand needle and purl it, k2 from cable needle, p2, k2*, rep from * to * twice more.

Change to 4mm (US 6, UK 8) needles.

Row 17: *k2, p2*, rep from * to * to last 3 sts, k2, p1.

Cast off.

MAKING UP
With RS facing, join the side seams using mattress stitch. Weave in all loose ends.

These useful cuffs will keep your hands warm on a winter's day, whether cycling, walking or working on a computer, as they allow you to have totally free hands. I have chosen a classic colour for this design and a gorgeous alpaca yarn, but they could equally well be knitted in a bright colour.

Versatile Mesh Headband

Materials:
» 1 ball of fingering (4-ply) silk/merino yarn in variegated cream and purple; 50g/246yd/225m

Needles:
» 3.25mm (US 3, UK 10) knitting needles

Instructions:

Cast on 57 sts.

Row 1: k1, *yfrn, k2tog, rep from * to end of row.

Row 2: purl.

Row 3: *sl1, k1, psso, yfrn, rep from * to last st, k1.

Row 4: purl.

Rep these 4 rows until work fits snugly when stretched around your head.

Cast off.

MAKING UP

With RS together, join seams together using mattress stitch. Weave in all loose ends.

This is a really versatile headband that can be worn in numerous ways – twist it, wrap it and play around to create the look you like. It is knitted with a silky, 4-ply variegated yarn in a lacy stitch to make it very flexible.

Love My Boot Cuffs

Materials:

CHILD'S SIZE:

» 2 balls of light worsted (DK/8-ply) pure alpaca yarn in red (A);
50g/109yd/100m

» 1 ball of worsted (aran/10-ply) textured yarn in white (B);
100g/138yd/125m

WOMAN'S SIZE:

» 1 ball of light worsted (DK/8-ply) pure alpaca yarn in red (C);
50g/109yd/100m

» 1 ball of worsted (aran/10-ply) textured yarn in dark green (D);
50g/138yd/125m

Needles:

» 5mm (US 8, UK 6) knitting needles

Instructions:

Make two.

CHILD'S SIZE

Using yarn A, cast on 48 sts.

Rows 1–18: *k2, p2*, rep from * to * to end of row.

Work the patterned section.

WOMAN'S SIZE

Using yarn C, cast on 60 sts.

Rows 1–22: *k2, p2*, rep to end of row.

Work the patterned section.

CHILD'S SIZE

Continue in yarn A.

Rows 1–4: st st starting with a knit row.

WOMAN'S SIZE

Continue in yarn A.

Rows 1–6: st st starting with a knit row.

BOTH SIZES

Using the chart, insert the heart motif. Note that you will be working from the top down so the heart is in the correct position once the boot cuff is on the leg.

Row 1: k3A, *k2B, k2A, k2B, k6A*; rep from * to * to last 9 sts, k2B, k2A, k2B, k3A.

Rows 2–8: follow the chart for these rows, ending with a purl row.

Rows 9 and 10: work st st.

Row 11: k1A, k1B, k10A, *k1B, k11A* rep to end.

Row 12: p10A, *p3B, p9A*, rep to last 14 sts, p3B, p8A, p3B.

Row 13: as row 11, cut off yarn B.

Rows 14–16: work st st in yarn A, starting with a purl row.

Row 17: cast off.

MAKING UP

Weave in all loose ends. With RS facing, use mattress stitch to join side seams of the pattern component of the boot cuff. Sew up rib on the rear side of the boot cuff.

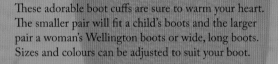

These adorable boot cuffs are sure to warm your heart. The smaller pair will fit a child's boots and the larger pair a woman's Wellington boots or wide, long boots. Sizes and colours can be adjusted to suit your boot.

Slouchy Hat

Materials:

» 1 ball each of worsted (aran/10-ply) wool/mohair blend yarn in teal (A) and grey (B); 100g/126yd/115m

Tools:

» 7mm (US 10½, UK 2) circular knitting needle, 16in (40cm) long

» 7mm (US 10½, UK 2) DPN

» 2 stitch markers

Gauge (tension):

» 14 sts x 18 rows = 4in (10cm) square using 7mm (US 10½, UK 2) circular needle over st st

Instructions:

Using 7mm (US 10½, UK 2) circular needle and yarn A, cast on 65 sts. Place a stitch marker to denote start of each round. Join the round, being careful not to twist any stitches. Slip marker as you pass it on each round.

Round 1: knit.

Round 2: purl.

Repeat rounds 1 and 2 four more times, then repeat round 1 once. Change to yarn B.

Rounds 12–22: knit.

Change to yarn A.

Rounds 23, 25, 27, 29: knit.

Rounds 24, 26, 28, 30: purl.

Repeat rounds 12–30 twice more.

Cut off yarn A and change to yarn B.

Next round: *k13, place marker (using a different colour from the marker used to denote start of each round), rep from * to end of round. Change to DPN when work becomes too tight on circular needle.

DECREASING FOR CROWN

Next row: k2tog, *knit to 2 sts before marker, k2tog, slip marker, k2tog, rep from * four times, k to last 2 sts, k2tog (55 sts).

Rep last round (decreasing 10 sts per round) until 25 sts remain. Cut yarn and, using a needle, thread it through rem sts and draw them up tightly to fasten off.

MAKING UP

Pull yarn up tightly and fasten off securely.

Rooster Snood

Materials:
» 1 ball each of light worsted (DK/8-ply) alpaca/merino yarn in gooseberry (A), damson (B), red (C) and cream (D); 50g/124yd/113m

Tools:
» 4.5mm (US 7, UK 7) circular knitting needle
» Stitch marker

Size:
» Circumference: 26in (66cm), height: 10¼in (26cm)

Gauge (tension):
» 23 sts x 29 rows = 4in (10cm) using 4.5mm (US 7, UK 7) circular needle over Fair Isle pattern

Instructions:

Using yarn A, cast on 150 sts. Place a stitch marker to denote start of each round. Join the round, being careful not to twist any stitches. Slip marker as you pass it on each round.

Rounds 1 and 2: using yarn A, knit.

Round 3: *k2B, k1A, rep from * to end of round.

Rounds 4 and 5: *k2A, k1B, rep from * to end of round.

Round 6: *k2B, k1A, rep from * to end of round.

Rounds 7 and 8: using yarn A, knit.

Fasten off yarns A and B.

Rounds 9 and 10: using yarn C, knit.

Round 11: *k2D, k3C, rep from * to end of round.

Rounds 12 and 13: k3D, *k1C, k4D, rep from * to last 2 sts, k1C, k1D.

Round 14: *k2D, k3C, rep from * to end of round.

Rounds 15 and 16: using yarn C, knit.

Rounds 17–24: work as rounds 1–8, reversing the yarn colours.

Rounds 25–32: work as rounds 9–16.

Work rounds 1–32 once more.

Rounds 65–72: work as rounds 1–8.

Cast off using yarn A.

MAKING UP

Press snood lightly. Weave in all loose ends.

> This simple Fair Isle snood works by using combinations of colours that are interchangeable. The snood is knitted in the round.

Steely Tweed Scarf

Materials:
» 9 balls of light worsted (DK/8-ply) yarn: 4 in mid grey (A), 4 in cream (B) and 1 in black (C); 50g/144yd/132m

Tools:
» 5mm (US 8, UK 6) knitting needles
» 5mm (US 8/H, UK 6) crochet hook
» CD case

Instructions:

Throughout the pattern, knit one strand of yarn A and one strand of yarn B together to produce the tweed effect.

Using one strand each of yarns A and B, cast on 45 sts, then ktbl to form a neat edge.

SCARF PATTERN

Rows 1 and 3: p3, *k1, sl1, k1, p3*, repeat from * to * to end of row.
Rows 2 and 4: *k3, p1, k1, p1*, repeat from * to * to last 3 sts, k3.
Rows 5 and 7: k4, *sl1, k5*, repeat from * to * to last 4 sts, k4.
Rows 6 and 8: p4, *k1, p5*, repeat from * to * to last 4 sts, p4.
Next rows: continue knitting rows 1–8 until scarf measures 66½in (169cm). Cast off. Weave in all loose ends.

MAKING UP

Using yarn C, wind it around the short sides of the CD case and cut it in the centre to make lengths for the tassels. Use four strands at a time and a 5mm (US 8/H, UK 6) crochet hook to thread the wool through the scarf to make 17 tassels for each end.

A classic look that is knitted by using shades of alpaca wool together. Black tassels add interest.

Frosty Wrist Warmers

Materials:

» 1 ball each of light worsted (DK/8-ply) merino yarn in red (A), white (B) and black (C); 100g/273yd/250m

Needles:

» 4mm (US 6, UK 8) knitting needles

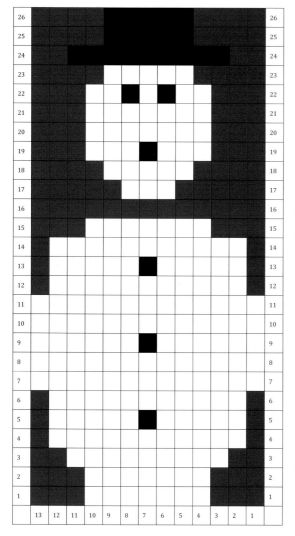

Instructions:

Make two. The black yarn is used double throughout to accentuate the snowman's hat and buttons.

Using yarn A, cast on 40 sts, then ktbl to form a neat edge.

Rows 1–16: *k1, p1*, rep from * to * to end of row.

Rows 17 and 18: st st.

Row 19: k2A, *k1B, k4A*, rep from * to * to last pattern rep, k2A.

Row 20: p1A, *p3B, p2A*, rep from * to * to last pattern rep, p1A.

Row 21: *k2B, k1A, k2B*, rep from * to * to end of row.

Row 22: as row 20.

Row 23: as row 19. Cut off yarn B.

Rows 24–26: using yarn A, st st.

Row 27: work row 1 of the chart, placing the two snowmen motifs as follows: k7A, k7B, k12A, k7B, k7A to set the spacing, then continue to work rows 2–26 from chart. Cut off yarns B and C.

Next 2 rows: using yarn A, st st.

Next 2 rows: *k1, p1*, rep to end of row.

Cast off.

MAKING UP

With RS facing, use mattress stitch to join the side seams, 10cm (4in) from the wrist end and 5cm (2in) from the finger end. This will leave a gap for your thumb to go through. Weave in all loose ends.

Everyone loves snowmen. I have knitted the motif using intarsia to avoid large loops forming at the back of the work, and cut-off lengths of white and black yarn to make the knitting easier.

Dusky Headband

Materials:

» 1 ball of worsted (aran/10-ply) baby alpaca/merino yarn in dusky pink; 50g/103yd/94m
» 1 button (optional)

Needles:

» 5mm (US 8, UK 6) knitting needles
» 4mm (US 6, UK 8) knitting needles

Instructions:

Using 5mm (US 8, UK 6) needles, cast on 17 sts.

LITTLE FLAKES STITCH

This is worked on an uneven number of stitches.

Row 1: purl.
Row 2: knit.
Row 3: *make 3 sts from 1 st (knit, purl, knit all into the same st), p1, rep from * to last st, work 3 sts into the last st.
Row 4: p3, *k1, p3, rep from * to end of row.
Row 5: k3, *p1, k3, rep from * to end of row.
Row 6: as row 4.
Row 7: k3tog, *p1, k3tog, rep from * to end of row.
Row 8: p1, *k1, p1, rep from * to end of row.
Row 9: p1, *k1, p1, k1 all into the same st, p1, rep from * to end of row.
Row 10: k1, *p3, k1, rep from * to end of row.
Row 11: p1, *k3, p1, rep from * to end of row.
Row 12: as row 10.
Row 13: p1, *k3tog, p1, rep from * to end of row.
Row 14: k1, *p1, k1, rep from * to end of row.

Rep rows 3–14 until work is long enough to fit around your head when slightly stretched.

MAKING UP

With RS together, join the end seams using mattress stitch.

6-PETAL FLOWER (OPTIONAL)

Using 4mm (US 6, UK 8) needles, cast on 4 sts.
**Row 1 and every wrong side row: purl.
Row 2 (RS): *k1, inc1, rep from * to last st, k1 (7 sts).

Row 4: *k1, inc1, rep from * to last st, k1 (13 sts).
Row 6: knit.
Row 8: k5, sk2po, k5 (11 sts).
Row 10: k4, sk2po, k4 (9 sts).
Row 12: k3, sk2po, k3 (7 sts).
Row 13: purl.

Cut yarn leaving a reasonable length and leave the 7 sts on the needle.

On the second needle, cast on 4 sts and rep from ** five more times (six petals in total), leaving RS facing for the next row (42 sts in total on needle).

Continue as follows:

Row 14 (RS): k6, k2tog, *k5, k2tog, rep from * three more times, k6 (37 sts).
Row 15: *p2tog, rep from * to last st, p1 (19 sts).
Row 16: knit.
Row 17: *p2tog, rep from * to last st, p1 (10 sts).
Row 18: *k2tog, rep from * to end of row (5 sts).
Row 19: pass second, third, fourth and fifth sts over the first stitch.

Cut yarn, and pass through remaining st.

MAKING UP

Pull up ends at the base of each petal and then, using each end in turn, sew adjacent petals together to approximately ½in (1.5cm) from the base. Weave in all loose ends. Sew the button onto the centre of the flower and then sew the flower onto the headband. Attach the tips of the top and bottom petals to the headband to prevent the flower flopping over.

This textured headband is made from a super soft yarn in a subtle colour. I have added a flower for fun and to give it a vintage look.

Allure Boot Cuffs

Materials:

» 1 ball each of worsted (aran/10-ply) yarn in black (A) and white (B); 100g/144yd/132m

Needles:

» 5mm (US 8, UK 6) knitting needles
» 5.5mm (US 9, UK 5) knitting needles

Instructions:

Make two.

Using 5mm (US 8, UK 5) needles and yarn A, cast on 54 sts.

Row 1: *k2, p2* rep to last 2 sts, k2.

Row 2: *p2, k2* rep to last 2 sts, p2.

Rows 3–22: rep rows 1 and 2 ten more times.

PATTERN

To set the pattern: using yarn A, purl, decreasing 1 stitch on 26th stitch (53 sts on needle).

Row 1 (RS): using yarn B, (k1, sl1) five times; *k12, sl 1, (k1, sl1) four times* rep from * to * once more to last st, k1.

Row 2: using yarn B, (p1, sl1) five times, *p12, sl1 (p1, sl1) four times; rep from * to * once more to last st, p1.

Row 3: using yarn A, k2, sl1, (k1, sl1) three times; *k14, sl 1, (k1, sl1) three times*; rep from * to * once more to last 2 sts, k2.

Row 4: using yarn A, p2, sl1, (p1, sl1), three times; *p14, sl 1, (p1, sl1) three times* rep from * to * once more to last 2 sts, p2

Rows 5–20: rep rows 1–4 four more times.

Rows 21 and 22: rep rows 1 and 2 once more. Cut off yarn B.

Cast off using yarn A.

MAKING UP

Weave in all loose ends. With RS facing, use mattress stitch to join the side seams of the pattern component of the boot cuff. Sew up the rib on the rear side of the boot cuff.

These boot cuffs will add style to any boot. This pattern is suitable for a knitter with some experience. For a change, try knitting the cuff in colours that complement your favourite coat.

Santa Slouch Hat

Materials:

» 3 balls of worsted (aran/10-ply) alpaca/merino yarn; 1 in cream (A) and 2 in red (B); 50g/103yd/94m

» Cardboard for pompom

Tools:

» 5mm (US 8, UK 6) DPN

» 5mm (US 8, UK 6) circular knitting needle, 16in (40cm) long

» Stitch marker

Gauge (tension):

» 18 sts x 24 rows = 4in (10cm) square using 5mm (US 8, UK 6) circular needle over st st

MAKING UP

Using yarn A, make a large pompom. Sew the pompom to the tip of the cast-off end.

STRIPED HAT VERSION

Work as for the red and cream hat in chosen colours and stripes of either 8 or 10 rows until you have 6 sts remaining.

OPTIONAL: Make three i-cords. Using 5mm (US 8, UK 6) DPN, arrange 3 sts on each needle and work each i-cord separately as follows: *knit 3 sts, slide to other end of needle without turning work; rep from * until 14 rows have been worked. Cast off. Rep for remaining i-cords. Attach the i-cords to the tip of the cast-off end. Weave in all loose ends.

Instructions:

Using 5mm (US 8, UK 6) circular needle and yarn A, cast on 87 sts and place a stitch marker to denote start of each round. Join the round being careful not to twist any stitches. Slip marker as you pass it on each round.

Rounds 1–9: purl.

Cut off yarn A and continue using yarn B.

Knit every round until work measures 5½in (14cm).

DECREASING FOR CROWN

Next round: *k27, sl 1, k1, psso, rep from * to end of round (84 sts).

Next 2 rounds: knit.

Next round: *k26, sl 1, k1, psso, rep from * to end of round (81 sts).

Next 2 rounds: knit.

Continue decreasing as above (3 sts on every decrease row) until you find it hard to work on circular needles.

Change to DPN, dividing your sts evenly across them and continue decreasing as above on every third row until you have 6 sts remaining.

Cut yarn and, using a needle, thread it through rem sts to draw them up tightly and fasten off.

Purple Mist Snood

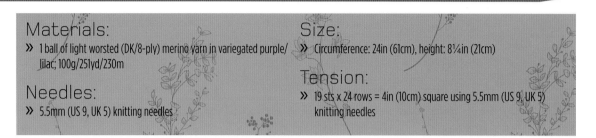

Materials:
» 1 ball of light worsted (DK/8-ply) merino yarn in variegated purple/lilac; 100g/251yd/230m

Needles:
» 5.5mm (US 9, UK 5) knitting needles

Size:
» Circumference: 24in (61cm), height: 8¼in (21cm)

Tension:
» 19 sts x 24 rows = 4in (10cm) square using 5.5mm (US 9, UK 5) knitting needles

Instructions:

Cast on 41 sts, then ktbl to form a neat edge.

Row 1: k3, p2, *k1, p1, k1, p4, repeat from * to last 8 sts, k1, p1, k1, p2, k3.

Row 2: k3, k2, *p1, k1, p1, k4, repeat from * to last 8 sts, p1, k1, p1, k5.

Row 3: k3, p2, *kfbf, p1, kfbf, p4, rep from * to last 8 sts, kfbf, p1, kfbf, p2, k3.

Row 4: k3, k2, *p3tog, k1, p3tog, k4, rep from * to last 8 sts, p3tog, k1, p3tog, k5.

Repeat rows 1–4 until work measures approximately 24in (61cm). Cast off, leaving a long yarn tail for sewing up your work.

MAKING UP
Press snood lightly. With RS facing, join cast-on and cast-off ends using mattress stitch. Weave in all loose ends.

This is a very simple, textured snood that only uses one ball of a lovely variegated yarn.

Candy Stripe Scarf

Materials:
» 5 balls of light worsted (DK/8-ply) yarn: 2 in midnight blue (A), 2 in rose (B) and 1 in cream (C); 50g/144yd/132m

Needles:
» 3.75mm (US 5, UK 9) knitting needles

KNITTING NOTE
Twist the yarn every second row to avoid large loops forming as you knit the scarf.

Instructions:
Using yarn A, cast on 41 sts, then ktbl to form a neat edge.

SCARF PATTERN
Rows 1 and 2: work g st (knit every row).
Rows 3 and 4: work st st.
Rows 5–8: change to yarn B, work st st.
Rows 9 and 10: change to yarn C, work st st.
Rows 11–16: change to yarn A, work st st.
Rep rows 5–16 until work measures 44in (112cm), ending with a stripe in yarn C.
Next 2 rows: change to yarn A, work st st.
Next 4 rows: g st.
Cast off.

MAKING UP
Weave in all loose ends.

I have knitted this scarf for a child but the pattern can be adjusted to fit an adult. Colours can be chosen to suit your preferences.

Playful Wrist Warmers

Materials:
» 2 balls of light worsted (DK/8-ply) super fine alpaca yarn in cream; 100g/273yd/250m
» 2 black buttons

Needles:
» 4.5mm (US 7, UK 7) knitting needles
» 5mm (US 8, UK 6) knitting needles
» 1 cable needle

Instructions:

Make two. The yarn is used double throughout.

Using 4.5mm (US 7, UK 7) needles, cast on 34 sts, then ktbl to form a neat edge.

Rows 1 and 2: *k1, p1*, rep from * to * to end of row.

Change to 5mm (US 8, UK 6) needles and start 12-row pattern; inc 1 st at beginning and 1 st at end of the first row only (36 sts).

Rows 1 and 11: *k3, p1, k1, p1, k1, p1, k1*, rep from * to * to end of row.

Rows 2, 10 and 12: *k1, p1, k1, p1, k1, p1, p3*, rep from * to * to end of row.

Row 3: *k3, slip 3 sts onto a cable needle and place at front of work, k1, p1, k1, then p1, k1, p1 from cable needle*, rep from * to * to end of row.

Rows 4, 6 and 8: *p1, k1, p1, k1, p1, k1, p3*, rep from * to * to end of row.

Rows 5 and 7: *k3, k1, p1, k1, p1, k1, p1*, rep from * to * to end of row.

Row 9: *k3, slip next 3 sts onto a cable needle and place at front of work, p1, k1, p1, then k1, p1, k1 from cable needle*, rep from * to * to end of row.

Rep rows 1–12, then rep rows 1–10 once more.

Change to 4.5mm (US 7, UK 7) needles.

Decrease by k2tog evenly across the next row. The decreases take place on the first row of the final rib only.

Next row (wrist end): *k1, p1* rep from * to * to end of row.

Rep above row once more, then cast off.

MAKING UP

With RS facing, use mattress stitch to join the side seams, 2in (5cm) from the finger end and 2 3/8in (6cm) from the wrist end. Using spare yarn, add a button to embellish each wrist cuff. Weave in all loose ends.

These cuffs combine a panel of stocking stitch with a crossover textured moss stitch. Knit them in a colour of your choice and customize them by adding a button.

Alice Flora Headband

Materials:
» 1 ball each of superwash merino fingering (4-ply) yarn in pink (A), purple (B), green (C) and cream (D); 50g/137yd/125m

Needles:
» 3mm (US 2, UK 11) knitting needles
» 3.5mm (US 4, UK 9 or 10) knitting needles

KNITTING NOTE
I have knitted the flowers using two colours and alternating them. You can use just one colour if you prefer.

Instructions:

Using size 3mm (US 2, UK 11) needles and yarn A, cast on 107 sts.
Row 1: knit, cut off yarn A.
Change to 3.5mm (US 4, UK 9) needles.
Rows 2 and 3: st st using yarn B.
Row 4: now set pattern as follows for row 1 of chart with spacing in between the flowers:
k1B, *k1C, k7B, k1C, k3B* rep from * to * to last 10 sts, k1C, k7B, k1C, k1B.
Now work the next 12 rows from the chart starting with a purl row, noting the knit rows (odd numbers) are worked from right to left and the purl rows are worked from left to right. Cut off yarns A and C.
Rows 17 and 18: st st using yarn B, starting with a purl row.
Cut off yarn B and rejoin yarn A. Change to 3mm (US 2, UK 11) needles.
Row 19: knit.
Row 20: cast off knitwise.

MAKING UP
Weave in all loose ends. With RS facing, join side seams together using mattress stitch.

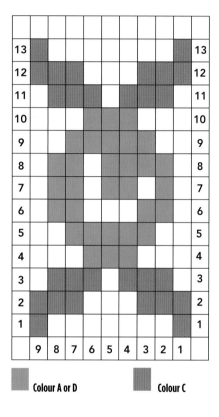

Colour A or D   Colour C

This headband has been made for a five- to eight-year-old child but can easily be adapted to fit an adult. The pattern for the Flossie Flower headband, top left of the photograph, can be found on page 168.

Imperium Boot Cuffs

Materials:

» 3 balls of super bulky (super chunky) yarn in blue; 100g/36yd/33m

Tools:

» 10mm (US 15, UK 000) circular knitting needle, 23½in (60cm) long
» 1 stitch marker

Instructions:

Make two.

Cast on 33 sts loosely. Place marker on right needle (this is to mark the beginning of the round).

Slip the first cast-on stitch to left-hand needle, then knit this slipped stitch together with the last cast-on stitch. You will now have 32 sts on your needle. Remember to move the marker at the end of each round.

Rows 1–24: *k1, p1* rep from * to * to end of row.

Cast off loosely following rib pattern.

MAKING UP

Weave in all loose ends.

A great, simple pattern makes these cuffs perfect to keep feet snug while you are hard at work in the garden. Try making them in green to make a handsome complement to traditional Wellington boots.

Winter Thyme Beanie

Materials:
» 1 ball each of worsted (aran/10-ply) pure wool in grey (A), lime (B) and purple (C); 100g/174yd/160m

Needles:
» 4.5mm (US 7, UK 7) knitting needles

Gauge (tension):
» Tension over st st: 20 sts x 22 rows = 4in (10cm) square using 4.5mm (UK 7, US 7) needles over st st

Instructions:

BOTTOM BAND
Using yarn A, cast on 14 sts then ktbl to form a neat edge.

Row 1 (WS): using yarn B, purl.
Row 2 (RS): using yarn B, knit.
Rows 3 and 4: using yarn A knit.
Row 5: using yarn C, purl.
Row 6: using yarn C, knit.
Rows 7 and 8: using yarn A, knit.
Row 9: using yarn B, purl.
Row 10: using yarn B, knit.
Rows 11 and 12: using yarn A, knit.
Rows 13–24: as rows 1–12.
Rows 25–28: as rows 5–8.
Rows 29–32: as rows 1–4.
Rows 33–36: as rows 9–12.
Rows 37–40: as rows 5–8.
Rows 41 and 42: as rows 1 and 2.
Continue repeating rows 3–42 until band measures 22in (56cm).
Cast off.

MAIN BODY
Fold band in half lengthwise, with WS together. With RS facing and yarn C, pick up and knit 97 sts across the top edge of folded band ensuring that sts are picked up from the front and the back in each stitch (this joins the band).
Next row: using yarn C, knit.
Cut off yarn C.
Rows 1–4: work 4 rows in st st using yarn A.

Row 5: k15A, k3B, k17A, k3B, k14A, k3B, k15A, k3B, k15A, k3B, k6A.
Row 6: p5A, p7B, p11A, p7B, p11A, p7B, p10A, p7B, p11A, p7B, p14A.
Row 7: k15A, k8B, k7A, k8B, k9A, k8B, k10A, k8B, k10A, k8B, k6A.
Row 8: p6A, p9B, p9A, p9B, p9A, p9B, p8A, p9B, p5A, p9B, p15A.
Row 9: k16A, k8B, k5A, k8B, k9A, k8B, k10A, k8B, k10A, k8B, k7A.
Row 10: p8A, p8B, p10A, p8B, p10A, p8B, p9A, p8B, p3A, p8B, p17A.
Row 11: k18A, k7B, k3A, k7B, k10A, k7B, k11A, k7B, k11A, k7B, k9A.
Row 12: p10A, p6B, p12A, p6B, p12A, p6B, p11A, p6B, p3A, p6B, p6A, p5B, p8A.
Row 13: k6A, k10B, k5A, k4B, k3A, k4B, k13A, k4B, k14A, k4B, k14A, k4B, k12A.
Row 14: p15A, p1B, p17A, p1B, p17A, p1B, p16A, p1B, p3A, p1B, p7A, p12B, p5A.
Row 15: k4A, k14B, k7A, k1B, k1A, k1B, k16A, k1B, k17A, k1B, k17A, k1B, k16A.
Cut off yarn A.
Row 16: p16C, p1B, p17C, p1B, p16C, p1B, p18C, p1B, p1C, p1B, p7C, p15B, p3C.
Cut off yarn C.
Row 17: as row 15.
Row 18: as row 14.
Row 19: as row 13.
Row 20: as row 12.
Row 21: as row 11.
Row 22: as row 10.
Row 23: as row 9.
Row 24: as row 8.

Row 25: as row 7.
Row 26: as row 6.
Row 27: as row 5.
Cut off yarn B.
Continue hat using yarn A only.
Row 28: purl, decreasing 1 st in middle of row (96 sts).

DECREASING FOR CROWN
Row 29: *k10, k2tog, rep from * to end (88 sts).
Row 30: purl.
Row 31: *k9, k2tog, rep from * to end (80 sts).
Row 32: purl.
Row 33: *k8, k2tog, rep from * to end (72 sts).
Row 34: purl.
Row 35: *k7, k2tog, rep from * to end (64 sts).
Row 36: purl.
Row 37: *k6, k2tog, rep from * to end (56 sts).
Row 38: purl.
Row 39: *k5, k2tog, rep from * to end (48 sts).
Row 40: purl.
Row 41: *k4, k2tog, rep from * to end (40 sts).
Row 42: purl.
Row 43: *k3, k2tog, rep from * to end (32 sts).
Row 44: purl.
Row 45: *k2, k2tog, rep from * to end (24 sts).
Row 46: purl.
Row 47: *k1, k2tog, rep from * to end (16 sts).
Row 48: purl.
Cut yarn and thread through rem sts.

MAKING UP
Pull yarn up tightly and fasten off securely.
Join back seam using mattress stitch.

Ophelia Snood

Materials:
» 1 ball of lace weight (2-ply) alpaca/silk yarn in rust; 100g/874yd/800m

Needles:
» 3.5mm (US 4, UK 9 or 10) knitting needles

Size:
» Circumference: 26in (66cm), height: 18½in (47cm)

Gauge (tension):
» 20 sts x 31 rows = 4in (10cm) square using 3.5mm (US 4, UK 9 or 10) needles over pattern

Instructions:

Cast on 104 sts then ktbl to form a neat edge.

Row 1 (RS): knit.

Row 2 and every even row: purl.

Row 3: knit.

Row 5: *k4, k2tog, yfwd, k1, yfwd, sl 1, k1, psso, k4, rep from * to end of row.

Row 7: *k3, k2tog, yfwd, k3, yfwd, sl 1, k1, psso, k3, rep from * to end of row.

Row 9: *k2, (k2tog, yfwd) twice, k1, (yfwd, sl 1, k1, psso) twice, k2, rep from * to end of row.

Row 11: *k1, (k2tog, yfwd) twice, k3, (yfwd, sl 1, k1, psso) twice, k1, rep from * to end of row.

Row 13: *(k2tog, yfwd) three times, k1, (yfwd, sl 1, k1, psso) three times, rep from * to end of row.

Row 14: purl.

Rep these 14 rows until work measures approximately 26in (66cm) ending with row 14.

Cast off, leaving a long yarn tail for sewing up your work.

MAKING UP

Press snood lightly. Join cast-off and cast-on ends with RS facing using mattress stitch. Weave in all loose ends.

Choose your favourite colour to knit this light and pretty snood, which has a delicate lace design.

Ribbed Scarf

Materials:
» 5 balls of worsted (aran/10-ply) yarn in variegated blue/orange; 100g/137yd/126m

Needles:
» 5.5mm (US 9, UK 5) knitting needles
» 5.5mm (US 9/I, UK 5) crochet hook

Instructions:
Cast on 50 sts, then ktbl to form a neat edge.

SCARF PATTERN
Row 1: *k2, p2*, repeat from * to * to last 2 sts, k2.
Row 2: *p2, k2*, repeat from * to * to last 2 sts, p2.
Rep rows 1 and 2 until work measures approximately 70¾in (180cm).
Cast off.

MAKING UP
Weave in all loose ends. To make the tassels, cut 81 lengths of yarn that are approximately 10¼in (26cm) long. Using your crochet hook to find the centre of the raised part of each section of the rib, thread three doubled strands of yarn through to make each tassel (you will have 27 tassels in total). Neaten up the tassels with scissors to ensure that they are all the same length.

This is a really simple scarf to make once you have mastered the skills of purl and plain knitting. I have used a fairly chunky variegated yarn to make the texture more effective.

Heathland Wrist Warmers

Materials:
» 1 ball of light worsted (DK/8-ply) merino yarn in variegated pink-green; 100g/232yd/212m

Needles:
» 3.5mm (US 4, UK 9 or 10) knitting needles
» 4mm (US 6, UK 8) knitting needles

Instructions:

Make two.

Using size 3.5mm (US 4, UK 9 or 10) needles, cast on 40 sts, then ktbl to form a neat edge.

Rows 1 and 2: knit.

Change to 4mm (US 6, UK 8) needles.

MAIN PATTERN

Row 1: knit, inc 3 sts evenly across the row (43 sts).

Row 2 and all even-numbered rows: work each st as it appears from this side of the work (i.e. knit the k sts and purl the p sts). Purl the loops made in the row below.

Rows 3, 11 and 13: knit.

Rows 5, 7 and 9: p1, *yfrn, k4, sl1, k1, psso, p1, k2tog, k4, yfrn, p1*, rep from * to * to end of row.

Rows 15, 17 and 19: p1, *k2tog, k4, yfrn, p1, yfrn, k4, sl1, k1, psso, p1*, rep from * to * to end of row.

Rep rows 1–20 twice.

Next rows: change to 3.5mm (US 4, UK 9 or 10) needles and rep rows 1 and 2. On row 2, dec 3 sts evenly across the row (40 sts).

Cast off using the picot cast-off as follows: cast off 2 sts, *slip stitch on right-hand needle on to left-hand needle, cast on 2 stitches using cable method, cast off 4 sts*. Rep from * to * to end of row. Fasten off last stitch.

MAKING UP

Join side seams 2in (5cm) from the top (picot edge) and 2¾in (7cm) from the bottom. This will leave a gap for your thumb to go through. Weave in all loose ends.

These pretty cuffs were inspired by the beautiful colours of a silky variegated yarn I found. The tones remind me of a visit to Scotland, where I saw the lovely hues of the heathers and ferns.

Forties-style Headband

Materials:

» 2 balls of light worsted (DK/8-ply) superfine alpaca yarn in cream; 50g/131yd/120m

Needles:

» 4mm (US 6, UK 8) knitting needles

Instructions:

Cast on 28 sts.

Row 1: knit.

Row 2: k11tbl, turn.

Rows 3 and 5: knit.

Row 4: k22tbl, turn.

Row 6: ktbl to end of row.

Row 7: k1, inc1 in next st, knit to last 3 sts, k2tog, k1.

Rep rows 6 and 7 until piece measures 9¾in (25cm) at the longest point, ending with row 6.

Now continue as follows:

Row 1: k1, (k2tog) thirteen times, k1 (15 sts).

Row 2: ktbl in every st.

Row 3: k1, inc1 in next st, knit to last 3 sts, k2tog, k1.

Rep rows 2 and 3 until work measures 24½in (62cm) at the longest edge, ending with row 2 of pattern.

Now continue as follows:

Row 1: k1, inc1 in each of the next 13 sts, k1 (28 sts).

Row 2: ktbl in every st.

Row 3: k1, inc1 in next st, knit to last 3 sts, k2tog, k1.

Rep rows 2 and 3 until work measures 32¼in (82cm) at the longest edge, ending with row 2 of pattern.

Next row: k22, turn.

Next row: ktbl in every st.

Next row: k11, turn.

Next row: ktbl in every st.

Cast off.

MAKING UP

After completing the knitting, block your work. Lay the headband flat with the underside facing you. Fold both side edges into the middle, starting from where the stitches are increased on one end and decreased on the other end, leaving the centre panel as a single piece of knitting. Press the sides lightly with an iron, so that the seam is down the middle of the band. Sew the seams together using mattress stitch. Weave in all loose ends. Finally, tie a knot (left end over right end, twist one end under and then right over left).

This headband is a replica of one that factory workers wore in the 1940s. It is knitted in a luxurious alpaca yarn.

Pig-in-the-Grass Boot Cuffs

Materials:

» 1 ball of worsted (aran/10-ply) wool/alpaca yarn in dark green (A); 100g/109yd/100m

» 1 ball of worsted (aran/10-ply) yarn in light pink (B); 100g/144yd/132m

Needles:

» 5.5mm (US 9, UK 5) knitting needles

» 5mm (US 8, UK 6) knitting needles

This bold cuff design is especially suited to adding character to wellies or wide-legged boots.

KNITTING NOTE

Twist the yarn every three to four sts to avoid long loops forming at the back of your work.

Instructions:

Make two.

Using 5.5mm (US 9, UK 5) needles and yarn A, cast on 58 sts then ktbl to form a neat edge.

Rows 1 and 2: st st.

PATTERN

Start reading the chart from the right-hand side.

Complete chart rows 1–20, starting with a knit row. Cut off yarn B. Change to size 5mm (US 8, UK 6) needles.

RIBBING

Row 1: *k2, p2* rep from * to * to last 2 sts, k2.

Row 2: *p2, k2* rep from * to * to last 2 sts, p2.

Rows 3–20: rep rows 1 and 2.

Row 21: as row 1.

Row 22: cast off leaving sufficient yarn to sew side seam.

MAKING UP

Weave in all loose ends. With RS facing, join the side seams of the pattern component of the boot cuff using mattress stitch. Sew up the rib on the rear side of the boot cuff.

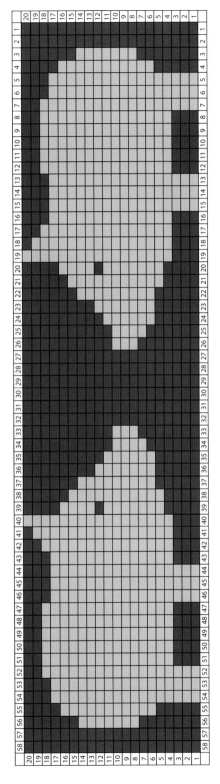

Striped-rim Fair Isle Hat

Materials:
» 1 ball each of fingering (4-ply) Shetland yarn in dark grey (A), light blue (B), light grey (C), variegated heather pink (D), light pink (E) and natural white (F); 25g/114yd/105m

Needles:
» 3mm (US 2, UK 11) knitting needles

Gauge (tension):
» 28 sts x 30 rows = 4in (10cm) square using 3mm (US 2, UK 11) needles over Fair Isle pattern

Instructions:

Using yarn A, cast on 120 sts then ktbl to form a neat edge.

Rows 1 and 2: using yarn B, knit.

Rows 3 and 4: using yarn B, *k2, p2, rep from * to end of row.

Rows 5–8: as rows 1–4 in yarn A.

Rows 9–24: rep rows 1–8 twice more.

Cut off yarn B. Start working from chart row 1 and, on this row only: k3, m1, *k6, m1, rep from * to last 3 sts, k3 (140 sts).

Continue working from chart until all 36 rows have been worked.

DECREASING FOR CROWN

Row 1: *k2A, k2C, k6A, k1C, k6A, k2C, k1A, rep from * to end of row.

Row 2: *p4C, p4A, s2ppC, p4A, p4C, p1A, rep from * to end of row (126 sts).

Row 3: *k2C, k1A, k2C, k2A, k2C, k1A, k2C, k2A, k2C, k1A, k1C, rep from * to end of row.

Row 4: *p1A, p3B, p2A, p1B, s2ppB, p1B, p2A, p3B, p1A, p1B, rep from * to end of row (112 sts).

Row 5: *k1A, k3B, k2A, k2B, k1A, k2B, k2A, k3B, rep from * to end of row.

Row 6: *p2B, p3A, p1B, s2ppB, p1B, p3A, p3B, rep from * to end of row (98 sts).

Row 7: *k2B, k3A, k2B, k1A, k2B, k3A, k1B, rep from * to end of row.

Row 8: *p4A, p1B, s2ppB, p1B, p4A, p1B, rep from * to end of row (84 sts).

Row 9: *k1B, k3A, k2B, k1A, k2B, k3A, rep from * to end of row.

Row 10: *p3A, p1B, s2ppB, p1B, p3A, p1B, rep from * to end of row (70 sts).

Row 11: *k1B, k2A, k2B, k1A, k2B, k2A, rep from * to end of row.

Row 12: *p2A, p1C, s2ppC, p1C, p2A, p1C, rep from * to end of row (56 sts).

Row 13: *k2A, k2C, k1A, k2C, k1A, rep from * to end of row.

Row 14: *p1A, p1C, s2ppC, p1C, p2A, rep from * to end of row (42 sts).

Row 15: *k1A, k2C, k1A, k2C, rep from * to end of row.

Row 16: *p1B, s2ppB, p1B, p1A, rep from * to end of row (28 sts).

Row 17: *k2B, k1A, k1B, rep from * to end of row.

Row 18: *s2ppC, k1A, rep from * to end of row (14 sts).

MAKING UP
Cut yarn and thread through remaining stitches. Pull yarn up tightly and fasten off securely. Join back seam using mattress stitch.

A
B
C
D
E
F

	4	3	2	1	

Blossom Snood

Materials:
» 8 balls of light worsted (DK/8-ply) alpaca/merino yarn: 2 in smoky blue (A), 2 in dusky pink (B), 2 in green (C) and 2 in shocking pink (D); 50g/127yd/116m

Needles:
» 7mm (US 10½, UK 2) knitting needles

Size:
» Circumference: 59¾in (152cm), height: 10¾in (27cm)

Tension:
» 16 sts x 16 rows = 4in (10cm) square using 7mm (US 10.5, UK 2) needles

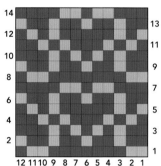

Key: A B C D

Chart A

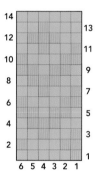

Instructions:

NOTE: yarn is held doubled throughout.
Using yarn A, cast on 40 sts then ktbl to form a neat edge.

SECTION A
Row 1 (RS): using yarn A, knit.
Row 2: k2, purl to last 2 sts, k2.
Join yarn B. From now on the first and last 2 sts of each row are knitted in the main colour for the section, to give a g st edge.
Rows 3–16: keeping g st edge as set, work 14 rows from chart A over the middle 36 sts. The odd-numbered rows are worked from right to left and are knitted, the even-numbered rows are worked from left to right and are purled. The pattern is repeated three times across each row. Fasten off yarn B.
Row 17: knit.
Row 18: k2, purl to last 2 sts, k2.
Rows 19 and 20: knit.
Fasten off yarn A.

SECTION B
Row 1: using yarn C, knit.
Row 2: using yarn C, k2, purl to last 2 sts, k2.
Join yarn B.
Rows 3–16: keeping g st edge as set, work 14 rows from chart B over the middle 36 sts. The pattern is repeated six times across each row.
Fasten off yarn B.

Row 17: using yarn C, knit.
Row 18: using yarn C, k2, purl to last 2 sts, k2.
Rows 19 and 20: using yarn C, knit.
Fasten off yarn C.

SECTION C
Row 1: using yarn D, knit.
Row 2: using yarn D, k2, purl to last 2 sts, k2.
Join yarn A.
Rows 3–18: keeping g st edge as set, work 16 rows from chart C over the middle 36 sts. The pattern repeat (marked by green borders) is worked seven times across each row. The last st is worked in D.
Fasten off yarn A.
Row 19: using yarn D, knit.
Row 20: using yarn D, k2, purl to last 2 sts, k2.
Rows 21 and 22: using yarn D, knit.
Fasten off yarn D.
Repeat sections A, B and C another three times. Cast off, leaving a long yarn tail for sewing up your work.

MAKING UP
Press snood lightly. Join cast-on and cast-off edges using mattress stitch with RS facing. Weave in all loose ends.

Chart B

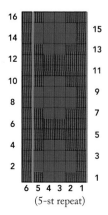

Chart C

(5-st repeat)

This is a fun snood to make and you can have a great time mixing and matching colours. The project uses a variety of Fair Isle designs.

Autumnal Stripes Scarf

Materials:

» 6 balls of light worsted (DK/8-ply) yarn: 2 in orange (A), 2 in red (B) and 2 in cream (C); 50g/144yd/132m

Needles:

» 4mm (US 6, UK 8) knitting needles

Instructions:

Using yarn A, cast on 50 sts then ktbl to form a neat edge.

SCARF PATTERN

Row 1: knit.

Row 2: purl.

Repeat rows 1 and 2 once more. Join in yarn B.

Rows 5–10: work st st in B. Join in yarn C.

Rows 11–14: work st st in C. Change to yarn B.

Rows 15–18: work st st in B. Change to yarn A.

Rows 19–22: work st st in A. Change to yarn C.

Rows 23–28: work st st in yarn C.

Rows 29–84: rep rows 1–28 twice more. Cut off yarns B and C.

Rows 85–98: work st st in yarn A, cut off yarn.

Rows 99–112: rejoin yarn B and work st st, cut off yarn.

Rows 113–126: rejoin yarn C and work st st, cut off yarn.

Next rows: rep the above sequence of 14-row sections (rows 85–126) seven more times and then one more stripe in yarn A.

Next rows: continue with the smaller stripes, ensuring they match the order of the ones worked at the start of the pattern (this will mean reversing the order). Start with 4 rows of yarn C.

At the end of the three repeats of the 28-row sequence, cast off.

MAKING UP

Weave in all loose ends.

This scarf is a welcome addition to any autumn/ winter wardrobe. I have used stripes to add interest. Choose bright colours or subtle colours to match your winter coat or jacket.

Parisienne Hand Warmers

Materials:
» 1 ball each of light worsted (DK/8-ply) yarn in lilac (A) and damson (B); 50g/131yd/120m

Needles:
» 4mm (US 6, UK 8) knitting needles

Instructions:

Make two.

FRILL
Row 1: using yarn A, cast on 2 sts.
Row 2: k1, m1, k1 (3 sts).
Row 3: p3.
Row 4: k1, m1, k1, m1, k1 (5 sts).
Row 5: k1, yo, k2tog, yo, k2tog.
Next rows: rep rows 1–5 seven more times (40 sts).

MAIN BODY OF WRIST WARMER
Rows 1 and 2: using yarn A, *k1, p1*, rep from * to * to end of row. Cut off yarn A.
Row 3: using yarn B, knit, increasing 1 st in the middle of the row (41 sts).
Rows 4–6: using yarn B and starting with a purl row, st st.
Rows 7–10: k1, *p1, k1*, rep from * to * to end of row.
Row 11: k1, *yfwd, sl1, k1, psso, k3, k2tog, yfwd, k1*, rep from * to * to end of row.
Row 12: purl.
Row 13: k2, *yfwd, sl1, k1, psso, k1, k2tog, yfwd, k3*, rep from * to * to last 7 sts, yfwd, sl1, k1, psso, k1, k2tog, yfwd, k2.
Row 14: purl.
Row 15: k3, *yfwd, sl1, k2tog, psso, yfwd, k5*, rep from * to * to last 6 sts, yfwd, sl1, k2tog, psso, yfwd, k3.
Row 16: purl.
Rep rows 7–16 four more times and then rows 7–10 once more. Cast off.

MAKING UP
When making up these wrist warmers, you will join the cast-off edge to the edge where the frill is. Note that the frill overlaps the seam. Using mattress stitch, join the side seam 2in (5cm) from the top, matching the cast-off edge to the start of the frill (where the colours change). Join the bottom of the cuff 3¾in (9.5cm) from the wrist end. This will leave a gap for your thumb to go through. Weave in all loose ends.

> This chic little pair of wrist warmers was inspired by a visit to Paris. They have a fun element as well as keeping your hands warm.

Two-tone Cable Headband

Materials:
» 1 ball of light worsted (DK/8-ply) Bluefaced Leicester in black-brown tweed yarn (A); 50g/112yd/102m
» 1 ball of light worsted (DK/8-ply) superfine alpaca yarn in black (B); 50g/131yd/120m

Needles:
» 4mm (US 6, UK 8) knitting needles
» 1 cable needle

Instructions:

Using yarn A, cast on 29 sts, then ktbl to form a neat edge.

NOTE: the first 10 and last 10 sts are worked in yarn A and the middle 9 sts in yarn B.

CABLE PATTERN

Remember to twist yarns every time you change colours to avoid gaps in your knitting.

Rows 1 and 5: k10A, k9B, k10A.

Rows 2, 4, 6 and 8: k1A, p9A, p9B, p9A, k1A.

Row 3: k1A, *slip next 3 sts onto a cable needle and hold at back of work, k3A, k3A from cable needle*, k3A, rep from * to * in yarn B, k3B, rep from * to * in yarn A, k4A.

Row 7: k4A, *slip 3 sts onto a cable needle and hold at front of work, k3A, k3A from cable needle*, k3B, rep from * to * in yarn B, k3A, rep from * to * in yarn A, k1A.

Continue the 8-row cable pattern until the headband fits snugly around your head with a slight stretch, ending on row 8 of pattern.

Next row: using yarn A, knit.

Cast off.

MAKING UP

With RS facing, join seams together using mattress stitch. Weave in all loose ends.

I have used a two-tone cable for this pattern to give it a certain panache. If preferred, it could be done in a single colour. This headband is particularly versatile and would suit all family members.

Clarice Boot Cuffs

Materials:
» 1 ball each of worsted (aran/10-ply) yarn in bright green (A), black (B), orange (C), and a small amount in light cream (D); 100g/144yd/132m

Needles:
» 5mm (US 8, UK 6) knitting needles

Instructions:

Make two.
Using yarn A, cast on 54 sts.
Rows 1–22: *k3, p3* rep from * to * end.

PATTERN SECTION
Use the chart, repeat sts 1–27 once to match your 54 sts on the needle. See chart note below for chequered repeat.
Row 17: knit.
Row 18: cast off.

MAKING UP
Weave in all loose ends. With RS facing, use mattress stitch to join the side seams of the pattern component of the boot cuff. Sew up the rib on the rear side of the boot cuff.

> **CHART NOTE**
> The two chequered borders continue with B and C in sequence across the row. All other lines do a complete pattern repeat from stitch 1.

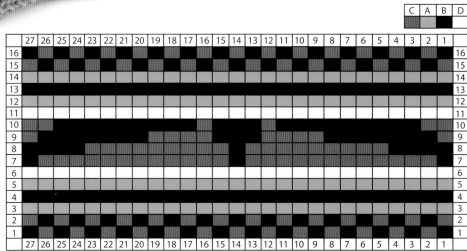

110

This design was inspired by my great love for Art Deco design. The bright colours will cheer you up on a winter's day.

Cable-knit Bobble Hat

Materials:

» 3 balls of worsted (aran/10-ply) alpaca/merino blend in light grey; 50g/103yd/94m

» Cardboard for pompom

Needles:

» 7mm (US 10½, UK 2) knitting needles

» 8mm (US 11, UK 0) knitting needles

» 1 cable needle

Gauge (tension):

» 20 sts x 22 rows = 4in (10cm) square using 4.5mm (US 7, UK 7) needles over st st with single strand of yarn

Instructions:

Using 7mm (US 10½, UK 2) needles and yarn doubled, cast on 74 sts, then ktbl to form a neat edge.

Rows 1–9: *k1, p1, rep from * to end of row.

Row 10: work 1 x 1 rib as in rows 1–9, increasing 1 st in middle of row (75 sts).

Change to 8mm (US 11, UK 0) needles.

MAIN BODY
CABLE AND DOT PATTERN

Row 1 (WS): *k2, k into front, back, front, back and front of next st (bobble made), k2, p2, k1, p2, k2, make bobble in next st as before, k2, rep from * to end of row.

Row 2: *p2, k5tog tbl (completing bobble), p2, C5F (sl 2 sts to cable needle and hold at front, k2, p1, k2 from cable needle), p2, k5tog tbl, p2, rep from * to end of row.

Row 3: *k5, p2, k1, p2, k5, rep from * to end of row.

Row 4: *p4, T3B, p1, T3F, p4, rep from * to end of row.

Row 5: *k4, p2, k3, p2, k4, rep from * to end of row.

Row 6: *p3, T3B, p3, T3F, p3, rep from * to end of row.

Row 7: *k3, p2, k2, make bobble in next st (as on first row), k2, p2, k3, rep from * to end of row.

Row 8: *p2, T3B, p2, k5tog tbl, p2, T3F, p2, rep from * to end of row.

Row 9: *k2, p2, k7, p2, k2, rep from * to end of row.

Row 10: *p1, T3B, p7, T3F, p1, rep from * to end of row.

Row 11: *k1, p2, k2, make bobble in next st, k3, make bobble in next st, k2, p2, k1, rep from * to end of row.

Row 12: *T3B, p2, k5tog tbl, p3, k5tog tbl, p2, T3F, rep from * to end of row.

Row 13: *p2, k11, p2, rep from * to end of row.

Row 14: *k2, p11, k2, rep from * to end of row.

Row 15: *p2, k3, make bobble in next st, k3, make bobble in next st, k3, p2, rep from * to end of row.

Row 16: *T3F, p2, k5tog tbl, p3, k5tog tbl, p2, T3B, rep from * to end of row.

Row 17: *k1, p2, k9, p2, k1, rep from * to end of row.

Row 18: *p1, T3F, p7, T3B, p1, rep from * to end of row.

Row 19: *k2, p2, k3, make bobble in next st, k3, p2, k2, rep from * to end of row.

Row 20: *p2, T3F, p2, k5tog tbl, p2, T3B, p2, rep from * to end of row.

Row 21: *k3, p2, k5, p2, k3, rep from * to end of row.

Row 22: *p3, T3F, p3, T3B, p3, rep from * to end of row.

Row 23: *k4, p2, k3, p2, k4, rep from * to end of row.

Row 24: *p4, T3F, p1, T3B, p4, rep from * to end of row.

DECREASING FOR CROWN

Row 25: k5, *p2tog, k1, p2tog, k4, k2tog, k4 rep from * to last 10 sts, p2tog, k1, p2tog, k5 (61 sts).

Row 26: p2, p2tog, p1, *k1, p1, k1, p2tog, p5, p2tog, rep from * to last 8 sts, k1, p1, k1, p2tog, p3 (51 sts).

Row 27: k1, *k3, k2tog, rep from * to end of row (41 sts).

Row 28: p1, *p2, p2tog, rep from * to end of row (31 sts).

Row 29: k1, *k1, k2tog, rep from * to end of row (21 sts).

Row 30: p1, *p2tog, rep from * to end of row (11 sts).

MAKING UP

Cut yarn and thread through rem sts. Pull yarn up tightly and fasten off securely. Join back seam using mattress stitch. Make one pompom and sew on top of hat (optional).

Graphite Snood

Materials:
» 8 balls of worsted (aran/10-ply) baby alpaca/merino yarn: 1 in light blue (A), 3 in cream (B), 1 in mint green (C), 1 in turquoise (D), 1 in dark blue (E) and 1 in pink (F); 50g/102yd/94m

Needles:
» 5mm (US 8, UK 6) knitting needles

Size:
» Circumference: 58in (148cm), height: 11½in (29cm)

Gauge (tension):
» 22 sts x 20 rows = 4in (10cm) square using 5mm (US 8, UK 6) needles over pattern

Instructions:

Using yarn A, cast on 60 sts then ktbl to form a neat edge.

Row 1: k3A, work row 1 from chart three times, k3B.

The odd-numbered rows are worked from right to left and are knitted, the even-numbered rows are worked from left to right and are purled.

Continue working from the chart, noting that the first and last 3 sts of every row (not shown on the chart) are knitted in the start and end colour, to form a g st edge, and the rest of the work is completed in st st.

Continue until work measures approximately 58in (148cm), finishing with last row of chart. Cast off, leaving a long yarn tail for sewing up your work.

MAKING UP

Press snood lightly. Join cast-on and cast-off ends using mattress stitch with RS facing. Weave in all loose ends.

Key:

A B C D E F

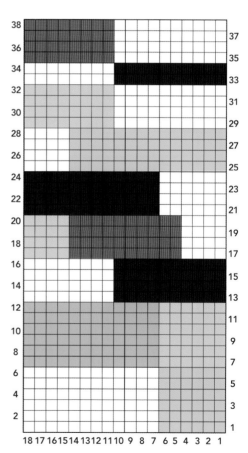

This is a great project for an evening. Simply choose your favourite colours in a soft yarn for a luxurious snood.

Autumn Haze Scarf

Materials:

» 3 balls of light worsted (DK/8-ply) silk blend yarn in variegated fawn-grey; 100g/295yd/270m

Needles:

» 7mm (US 10½, UK 2) knitting needles

Instructions:

Use the yarn tripled throughout the pattern.

Cast on 16 sts, then ktbl to form a neat edge.

SCARF PATTERN
Rows 1 and 2: *k2, p2*, rep from * to * to end.
Rows 3 and 4: *p2, k2*, rep from * to * to end.
Rep rows 1–4 until work measures approximately 61½in (156cm).
Cast off.

MAKING UP
Weave in all loose ends.

This is a really simple scarf that is made in variegated wool used triple, which adds texture to the stitch. The scarf uses a simple moss stitch knitted on large needles.

Bobble Tree Wrist Warmers

Materials:

» 2 balls of light worsted (DK/8-ply) yarn in rose; 50g/131yd/120m
» 23½in (60cm) length of elastic

Needles:

» 3.5mm (US 4, UK 9 or 10) knitting needles
» 4mm (US 6, UK 8) knitting needles

Instructions:

Make two. Using 3.5mm (US 4, UK 9 or 10) needles, cast on 40 sts, then ktbl to form a neat edge.

RIB

Rows 1 and 2: *k1, p1*, rep from * to * to end of row. On row 2 of rib, inc 1 st in the middle of the row (41 sts).

Change to 4mm (US 6, UK 8) needles.

MAIN PATTERN

Row 1 (RS): p2, *p6, k2tog, yfrn, p1, yo, sl1, k1, psso, p6*, p3, rep from * to * to last 2 sts, p2 (41 sts).

Row 2: k2, *k6, p1, k3, p1, k6*, k3, rep from * to * to last 2 sts, k2.

Row 3: p2, *p5, k2tog, yfrn, p3, yo, sl1, k1, psso, p5*, p3, rep from * to * to last 2 sts, p2.

Row 4: k2, *(k5, p1) twice, k5*, k3, rep from * to * to last 2 sts, k2.

Row 5: p2, *p4, k2tog, yfrn, (p1, k1) twice, p1, yo, sl1, k1, psso, p4*, p3, rep from * to * to last 2 sts, p2.

Row 6: k2, *k4, p1, k2, p1, k1, p1, k2, p1, k4*, k3, rep from * to * to last 2 sts, k2.

Row 7: p2, *p3, k2tog, yfrn, p2, k1, p1, k1, p2, yo, sl1, k1, psso, p3*, p3, rep from * to * to last 2 sts, p2.

Row 8: k2, *(k3, p1) twice, k1, (p1, k3) twice*, k3, rep from * to * to last 2 sts, k2.

Row 9: p2, *p2, k2tog, yfrn, p2, k2tog, yfrn, p1, yo, sl1, k1, psso, p2, yo, sl1, k1, psso, p2*, p3, rep from * to * to last 2 sts, p2.

Row 10: k2, *k2, (p1, k3) three times, p1, k2*, k3, rep from * to * to last 2 sts, k2.

Row 11 (bobble row): p2, *p2, (k1, p1, k1, p1) into next st, turn and p4, turn and k4, turn and p4, turn and sl1, k1, psso, k2tog, turn and p2tog, turn and slip bobble onto right-hand needle (bobble completed), p2, k2tog, yfrn, p3, yo, sl1, k1, psso, p2, make second

bobble and slip it onto right-hand needle, p2*, p3, rep from * to * to last 2 sts, p2.

Row 12: k2, *(k5, p1) twice, k5*, k3, rep from * to * to last 2 sts, k2.

These are the 12 rows of your pattern; rep them twice more.

Change to 3.5mm (US 4, UK 9 or 10) needles.

FINAL RIB

Row 1: *k1, p1*, rep from * to * to last 2 sts, p2tog.

Row 2: *k1, p1*, rep from * to * to end of row.

Cast off using the picot method as follows:

Cast off 2 sts, transfer 1 st on the right-hand needle to the left-hand needle, *cast on 2 sts using cable cast-on, cast off 4 sts*, rep from * to * to end of row, casting off any odd sts remaining.

MAKING UP

Using mattress stitch, join the seam 2½in (6.5cm) from the wrist end (cast-on edge) and 1½in (4cm) from the finger end. This will leave a gap for your thumb to go through. Sew the elastic around the picot edge end for a snug fit around the fingers.

Weave in all loose ends.

These very pretty, lacy cuffs are made from the softest alpaca. They can be knitted in colours of your choice to complement your favourite clothes.

Diamond Fair Isle Headband

Materials:

» 1 ball each of light worsted (DK/8-ply) alpaca/merino yarn in custard (A), smoky blue (B) and burnt orange (C); 50g/124yd/113m

Needles:

» 4mm (US 6, UK 8) knitting needles

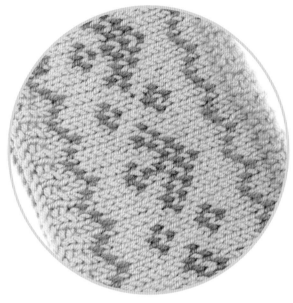

Instructions:

Using yarn A, cast on 112 sts.

Rows 1 and 2: *k1, p1, rep from * to end of row.

Rows 3 and 4: st st.

Row 5: *k3A, k1B, rep from * to end of row.

Row 6: *p1A, p1B, rep from * to end of row.

Row 7: k1A, *k1B, k3A, rep from * to last 3 sts, k1B, k2A.

Rows 8–10: work in st st in yarn A, starting with a purl row.

Row 11: k2A, *k1C, k5A, rep from * to last 2 sts, k1C, k1A.

Row 12: *p1C, p1A, p1C, p3A, rep from * to last 4 sts, p1C, p1A, p1C, p1A.

Row 13: k2A, k1C, *k3A, k1C, k1A, k1C, k1A, k1C, k3A, k1C, rep from * to last st, k1A.

Row 14: p4A, *p1C, p1A, p1C, p1A, p1C, p1A, p1C, p5A, rep from * to end of row.

Row 15: k4A, *k1C, k1A, k1C, k1A, k1C, k1A, k1C, k1A, k1C, k3A, rep from * to end of row.

Row 16: p4A, *p1C, p5A, rep from * to end of row.

Rows 17 and 19: as row 11.

Row 18: as row 12.

Rows 20–22: st st.

Rows 23–25: as rows 5–7.

Rows 26–27: st st, starting with a purl row.

Rows 28–29: *k1, p1, rep from * to end of row.

Cast off.

MAKING UP

With RS facing, join side seams together using mattress stitch. Weave in all loose ends.

The simplicity of the stitch and the spring-like colours used here really accentuate the Fair Isle pattern.

Bouclé Boot Cuffs

Materials:
» 1 ball each of worsted (aran/10-ply) textured yarn in cream (A), teal (B) and raspberry (C); 100g/138yd/125m

Needles:
» 5mm (US 8, UK 6) knitting needles
» 6mm (US 10, UK 4) knitting needles

Instructions:
Make two.
Using 5mm (US 8, UK 6) needles and yarn A, cast on 53 sts.

RIB
Row 1: *k2, p2*, rep from * to * to last st, k1.
Row 2: p1, *k2, p2*, rep from * to * to end of row.
Rows 3–12: rep rows 1 and 2.

MAIN BODY
Change to 6mm (US 10, UK 4) needles.
Row 1: k1 in yarn A. *Work 1 bobble in yarn B as follows: with B, k1, y/o, pass k st over y/o and return remaining y/o st to left needle, rep twice more, leaving last y/o st on right needle, k1 in yarn A*. Rep from * to * until end of row. Cut off yarn B.
Row 2: using yarn A, purl.
Row 3: using yarn C, work 1 bobble as above, *k1 in yarn A, work 1 bobble using yarn C*. Rep from * to * until end of row. Cut off yarn C.
Row 4: using yarn A, purl.
Rows 5–8: rejoin yarn B, knit every row (garter st).
Row 9: as row 3.
Row 10: as row 4.
Row 11: as row 1.
Row 12: as row 2.
Rows 13–16: rejoin yarn C, knit every row.
Cast off.

MAKING UP
Weave in all loose ends. With RS facing, use mattress stitch to join the side seams of the pattern component of the boot cuff. Sew up the rib on the rear side of the boot cuff.

The elongated bobbles give the yarn a bouclé effect and add character to the cuffs.

Chunky Rainbow Knit Hat

Materials:

» 1 ball each of bulky (chunky) 100% wool in blue (A), orange (B), mauve (C), yellow (D) and white (E); 50g/48yd/43m
» Card for pompom

Needles:

» 4.5mm (US 7, UK 7) knitting needles
» 5.5mm (US 9, UK 5) knitting needles
» Cable needle

Gauge (tension):

» 14 sts x 18 rows = 4in (10cm) square using 5.5mm (US 9, UK 5) needles over cable pattern

Instructions:

Using 4.5mm (US 7, UK 7) needles and yarn A, cast on 87 sts then ktbl to form a neat edge.

Rib row 1: *k2, p2, rep from * to last 3 sts, k2, p1.

Rib row 2: k1, p2, *k2, p2, rep from * to end of row.

Work rows 1 and 2 five more times.

Next row (RS): purl.

Next row (WS): k3, *kfb, k7, rep from * until last 4 sts, k4 (97 sts).

Change to yarn B and 5.5mm (US 9, UK 5) needles.

MAIN BODY: CABLE PATTERN

Row 1 (RS): p2, *k6, p2, k6, p5; repeat from * to end of row.

Row 2 and all alt rows: knit the knit stitches and purl the purl stitches as they present themselves.

Row 3: p2, *work 6 st right crossover as follows: slip 4 sts to cable needle and hold at back of work, k2, k4 from cable needle, p2; work 6 st left crossover as follows: slip 2 sts to cable needle and hold at front of work, k4, k2 from cable needle, p5, rep from * to end of row.

Row 5: p2, *k4, work 3 st left crossover as follows: slip 2 sts to cable needle and hold in front, p1, k2 from cable needle: work 3 st right crossover as follows: slip 1 st to cable needle and hold at back of work, k2, p1 from cable needle, k4, p5, rep from * to end of row.

Row 7: p2, *k4, p1, work 4 st crossover as follows: slip 2 sts to cable needle and hold at front of work, k2, k2 from cable needle, p1, k4, p5, rep from * to end of row.

Row 9: p2, *k4, work 3 st right crossover as follows: slip 1 st to cable needle and hold at back of work, k2, p1 from cable needle, work 3 st left cross-over as follows: slip 2 sts to cable needle and hold at front of work, p1, k2 from cable needle, k4, p5, rep from * to end of row.

Rep rows 3–10 of cable pattern once using yarn C and once using yarn D.

DECREASING FOR CROWN

Change to yarn E.

Row 1: p2, *k2, k2tog, k2, p2, k2, k2tog, k2, p5 (87 sts).

Row 2: *k2, k2tog, k1, p2, p2tog, p1, k2tog, p2, p2tog, p1, rep from * to last 2 sts, k2tog (66 sts).

Row 3: p1, *k1, k2tog, k1, p1, k1, k2tog, k1, p1, p2tog, p1, rep from * to end of row (51 sts).

Row 4: *k2tog, k1, p2tog, p1, k1, p2tog, p1, rep from * to last st, k1 (36 sts).

Row 5: p1, *k2tog, p1, k2tog, p2tog, rep from * to end of row (21 sts).

MAKING UP

Cut yarn and thread through rem sts. Pull yarn up tightly and fasten off securely. Join back seam using mattress stitch. Make one pompom using yarns B, C, D and E and sew on top of hat.

Adriatic Snood

Materials:
» 1 ball of lace weight (1–3-ply) baby alpaca/silk yarn in sparkly blue; 100g/984yd/800m

Tools:
» 4mm (US 6, UK 8) circular knitting needle
» Stitch marker

Size:
» Circumference: 27in (69cm), height: 9¼in (23.5cm)

Gauge (tension):
» 16 sts x 17 rows = 4in (10cm) square using 4mm (US 6, UK 8) needles over pattern

Instructions:

Cast on 109 sts, holding the yarn double throughout. Place a stitch marker to denote start of each round. Join the round, being careful not to twist any stitches. Slip marker as you pass it on each round.

Round 1: k1, *yo, k2tog, k2, rep from * to end of row.
Round 2: p1, *p2tog, yo, p2, rep from * to end of row.
Round 3: k3, *yo, k2tog, k2 rep from * to last 2 sts, yo, k2tog.
Round 4: p1, *yo, p2tog, p2, rep from * to end of row.
Round 5: k1, *k2tog, yo, k2, rep from * to end of row.
Round 6: p3, *yo, p2tog, p2, rep from * to last 2 sts, yo, p2tog.

Rep the above 6 rounds until work measures approximately 9¼in (23.5cm). Cast off.

MAKING UP
Press snood lightly. Weave in all loose ends.

This is a really pretty spring or summer snood knitted in a lace stitch to show off the sparkly elements of the yarn. The yarn is used double throughout and the snood fits once round the neck.

Red Rooster Scarf

Materials:
» 2 balls of worsted (aran/10-ply) yarn in red; (100g/144yd/132m)

Needles:
» 5.5mm (US 9, UK 5) knitting needles
» 1 cable needle

SPECIAL STITCHES
C6B: slip next 3 sts on to a cable needle and hold at back of work, knit next 3 sts from left-hand needle, then knit sts from cable needle.
C6F: slip next 3 sts on to a cable needle and hold at front of work, then knit next sts from left-hand needle.

Instructions:

Cast on 46 sts, then ktbl to form a neat edge.

DOUBLE CABLE PATTERN
Row 1: p5, k36, p5.
Row 2: k5, p36, k5.
Row 3: p5, c6b, c6f. Rep the 12-stitch cable pattern twice more, p5.
Row 4: k5, p36, k5.
Rows 5 and 6: as rows 1 and 2.
Repeat the above 6 rows until work measures 32¼in (82cm), then rep rows 1–4 once more. Cast off.

MAKING UP
Measure 4¾in (12cm) from the cast-on/cast-off edges. Using a piece of yarn, gather the end of the scarf in, and wrap the wool tightly around the middle several times. Tie a knot and sew in any loose ends. Fan your knitting out to form the edge.

MAKING THE BOW
Cast on 16 sts.
Rows 1–16: knit.
Cast off.
Fold knitting in half lengthways (short ends together). Using a tapestry needle and a piece of yarn, do a series of running sts along the centre line and draw them in tightly to form the centre of the bow. Weave in all loose ends.

COMPLETING THE SCARF
Cut six lengths of yarn, each measuring approximately 30in (76cm). Tie a knot at one end to hold the pieces together. Make a long plait using the strands in three pairs. Fold the completed plait in half and tie it around the centre of the bow. To wear the scarf, wrap it around your neck crossing the two ends over each other. Hold the bow over the centre and tie the plaits together.

This is a neat little scarf that will add fun and style to your wardrobe. For a different look change the central bow and add a large brooch. The scarf is easy to make once you have learnt how to cable.

Mondrian Wrist Warmers

Materials:

» 1 ball each of light worsted (DK/8-ply) merino yarn in red (A), yellow (C) and green (E); 100g/273yd/250m

» 1 ball each of light worsted (DK/8-ply) alpaca yarn in black (B) and white (D); 50g/131yd/120m

Needles:

» 4mm (US 6, UK 8) knitting needles

Instructions:

The yarn is used double throughout. Twist the yarn every 3 sts to avoid large loops forming across the back of your work.

RIGHT HAND

Using yarn A, cast on 40 sts, then ktbl to form a neat edge.

Rows 1–14: *k2, p2*, rep from * to * to end of row.

SHAPING FOR THUMB

Row 15: using yarn B, k20, m1, k5, m1, k15 (42 sts).

Row 16: purl.

The Mondrian-style colour blocks are done over 6 rows, so whether you are knitting or purling, the colour changes take place at the same point.

Row 17: k8C, k4B, k6D, k8B, k6C, k10B.

Row 18: purl, following the same colour sequence as row 17.

Row 19: k8C, k4B, k6D, k2B, m1, k6B, k1C, m1, k5C, k10B (44 sts).

Rows 20–22: st st, starting with a purl row, and following the same colour sequence as row 19.

Row 23: using yarn A, k20, m1, k9, m1, k15 (46 sts).

Row 24: purl.

Row 25: k8D, k4B, k16D, k3B, k8D, k4B, k3D.

Row 26: purl, following the same colour sequence as row 25.

Row 27: k8D, k4B, k8D, m1, k8D, k3B, m1, k8D, k4B, k3D (48 sts).

Rows 28–30: st st, starting with a purl row, and following the same colour sequence as row 27.

DIVIDE FOR THUMB

Row 31: using yarn B, (RS) k33, turn. Cut off yarn D.

Row 32: p13 using yarn B.

Rows 33–38: working on these 13 sts only, work 6 rows in st st, using yarn B.

Row 39: *k2, p2*, rep from * to * to last st, k1.

Row 40: p1, *k2, p2* rep from * to * to end of row.

Cast off.

Using a tapestry needle and mattress stitch, sew side seams of thumb together.

With RS facing and yarn B, rejoin yarn and pick up and knit 2 sts from base of thumb then knit to end of row (37 sts).

Row 42: purl, using yarn B.

Row 43: k15E, k5B, k6D, k4B, k7C.

Rows 44–48: starting with a purl row, st st, following the same colour sequence as row 43.

Rows 49 and 50: st st, using yarn A.

Row 51: k4B, k6D, k8C, k5B, k8D, k6C.

Rows 52–56: starting with a purl row, st st, following the same colour sequence as row 51. Cut off all yarns except yarn A.

Row 57: using yarn A, knit.

Row 58: *k2, p2*, rep from * to * to last st, k1.

Row 59: p1, *k2, p2*, rep from * to * to end of row.

Cast off following rib pattern of last 2 rows. Cut off yarn, leaving a sufficient length to sew up the side seam.

LEFT HAND

Work as for right hand to the thumb shaping.

Row 15: using yarn B, k15, m1, k5, m1, k20 (42 sts).

Row 16: purl.

Row 17: k10B, k6C, k8B, k6D, k4B, k8C (42 sts).

Row 18: purl, following the same colour sequence as row 17.

Row 19: k10B, k5C, m1, k1C, k6B, m1, k2B, k6D, k4B, k8C (44 sts).

Rows 20–22: st st, starting with a purl row, and following the same colour sequence as row 19.

Row 23: using yarn A, k15, m1, k9, m1, k20 (46 sts).

Row 24: purl.

Row 25: k3D, k4B, k8D, k3B, k16D, k4B, k8D (46 sts).

Row 26: purl, following the same colour sequence as row 25.

Row 27: k3D, k4B, k8D, m1, k3B, k8D, m1, k8C, k4B, k8D (48 sts).

Rows 28–30: st st, starting with a purl row and following the same colour sequence as row 27.

DIVIDE FOR THUMB

Row 31 (RS): using yarn B, k28, turn.

Row 32: p13.

Rows 33–40: work as for right hand from rows 33–40.

Cast off all sts. With RS facing, rejoin yarn and pick up and knit 2 sts from base of thumb, then knit to end of row (37 sts).

Row 42: using yarn B, purl.

Row 43: k7C, k4B, k6D, k5B, k15E.

Rows 44–48: st st, starting with a purl row and following the same colour sequence as row 43.

Rows 49–50: using yarn A, st st.

Row 51: k6C, k8D, k5B, k8C, k6D, k4B.

Rows 52–56: st st, starting with a purl row and following the same colour sequence as row 51. Cut off all yarns except yarn A.

Row 57: using yarn A, knit.

Row 58: *k2, p2*, rep from * to * to last st, k1.

Row 59: p1, *k2, p2*, rep from * to * to end of row.

Cast off following rib pattern of last 2 rows. Cut off yarn, leaving a sufficient length to sew up the side seam.

MAKING UP

Sew up side seams, with RS facing, using a tapestry needle and mattress stitch. Match the colours as you sew. Weave in all loose ends.

The geometric design of these gloves makes them rather eye-catching. They were inspired by an exhibition I saw featuring the Dutch artist, Mondrian, and are knitted using a Fair Isle technique combined with intarsia.

Cable Headband

Materials:
>> 1 ball of worsted (aran/10-ply) yarn in red (A); 50g/91yd/ 83m
>> 1 ball of worsted (aran/10-ply) yarn in variegated red and grey (B); 100g/182yd/166m

Needles:
>> 4mm (US 6, UK 8) knitting needles
>> 5mm (US 8, UK 6) knitting needles
>> 1 cable needle

Instructions:

Using 4mm (US 6, UK 8) knitting needles and yarn A, cast on 104 sts, then ktbl to form a neat edge.

Rows 1 and 2: *k1, p1, rep from * to end of row.

Cut off yarn A and join yarn B.

Row 3: p16, *inc1, p12, rep from * to last 16 sts, inc1, purl to end (111 sts).

Change to 5mm (US 8, UK 6) needles and insert honeycomb pattern as follows:

HONEYCOMB CABLE

This is worked over a multiple of 11 sts.

Rows 1 and 5: p2, *k8, p3, rep from * to last 10 sts, k8, p2.

Row 2 and all even-numbered rows: k2, *p8, k3, rep from * to last 10 sts, p8, k2.

Row 3: p2, *work left crossover on 4 sts as follows: slip 2 sts to cable needle and hold in front of work, k2, k2 from cable needle; work right crossover on 4 sts as follows: slip 2 to cable needle and hold in back of work, k2, k2 from cable needle, p3, rep from * to last 10 sts, left crossover, right crossover, p2.

Row 7: p2, *right crossover, left crossover, p3, rep from * to last 10 sts, right crossover, left crossover, p2.

Row 8: k2, *p8, k3, rep from * to last 10 sts, p8, k2.

Repeat the above 8-row pattern once and then the first 4 rows once. Cut off yarn B, join yarn A.

Change to 4mm (US 6, UK 8) needles.

Next row: k15, k2tog, *k11, k2tog, rep from * to last 16 sts, k to end of row (104 sts).

Next 2 rows: *k1, p1, rep from * to end of row.

Cast off.

MAKING UP

With RS facing and yarn A, sew up each rib using mattress stitch. Use yarn B to sew up the central panel. Weave in all loose ends.

This is a great headband for all the family. It will keep the chill away and looks great. It can be worn to walk, ski or cycle and its width makes it a great alternative to a hat, as it keeps your ears warm.

Blooming Boot Cuffs

Materials:

» 1 ball each of worsted (aran/10-ply) textured yarn in lilac (A) and cerise (B), and small amounts in light pink (C) and mid blue (D); 100g/138yd/125m

Needles:

» 5mm (US 8, UK 6) knitting needles

» 6mm (US 10, UK 4) knitting needles

KNITTING NOTE

After the rib, cut yarns A, C and D into lengths of approximately 79in (2m) to make the intarsia flowers more manageable.

Instructions:

Make two.

Using 5mm (US 8, UK 6) needles and yarn A, cast on 52 sts.

Rows 1–18: *k2, p2* rep from * to * to end of row. Cut off yarn A.

Rows 19 and 20: change to 6mm (US 10, UK 4) needles. Using yarn B, k to end.

Note: yarn B will now be the main colour for the rest of the boot cuff.

PATTERNED SECTION

Start working from the chart as follows:

Row 1: k6 yarn B, place first flower using yarn C; k8 yarn B, place second flower in yarn D; k8 yarn B, place third flower in yarn A, k6.

	13	12	11	10	9	8	7	6	5	4	3	2	1	
11														11
10														10
9														9
8														8
7														7
6														6
5														5
4														4
3														3
2														2
1														1
	13	12	11	10	9	8	7	6	5	4	3	2	1	

CENTRE OF FLOWERS

First flower: blue (yarn D)

Second flower: lilac (yarn A)

Third flower: light pink (yarn C)

Continue working from rows 2–11 of the chart.

Row 12: purl.

Row 13: knit.

Row 14: *k1, inc 1 (into the same stitch)*, rep to end of row. Cast off.

MAKING UP

Weave in all loose ends. With RS facing, use mattress stitch to join the side seams of the pattern component of the boot cuff. Sew up the rib on the rear side of the boot cuff.

A	B	D	

These cheerful cuffs will add a new lease
of life and originality to your boots,
whatever the length.

Ribbed Pompom Hat

Materials:
» 1 ball of worsted (aran/10-ply) variegated blue/tan yarn; 100g/138yd/126m
» Small amount of tan yarn in similar weight for pompoms

Tools:
» 5.5mm (US 9, UK 5) circular knitting needle, 16in (40cm) long
» 5.5mm (US 9, UK 5) crochet hook (optional for chain)
» Stitch marker

Gauge (tension):
» 15 sts x 24 rows = 4in (10cm) square using 5.5mm (US 9, UK 5) needles over rib pattern

Instructions:

Cast on 85 sts. Place a stitch marker to denote start of each round. Join the round being careful not to twist any stitches. Slip marker as you pass it at the end of each round.

All rounds: *k3, p2, rep from * to end.

Continue working rounds as above until work measures 7in (18cm).

SHAPING THE CROWN
Next round (dec): *k3, p2tog, rep from * to end of row (68 sts).
Next 3 rounds: *k3, p1, rep from * to end of row.
Next round (dec): *k1, k2tog, p1, rep from * to end of row (51 sts).
Next round: *k2tog, yo, p1, rep from * to end of round.
Next 9 rounds: *k2, p1, rep from * to end of row.
Next round: *k1, m1, rep from * to end of row (102 sts).
Next round: knit.
Next round: cast off.

MAKING UP
Using four strands of yarn, make a 10in (25cm) crochet chain or a chain using loops to thread through spaces in the crown of the hat. Make two pompoms in contrasting yarn (or the same colour if you prefer). Attach one pompom to each end of the chain once it has been threaded through the hat. Weave in all loose ends. Draw hat closed and tie knot in chain to secure.

Agincourt Snood

Materials:
» 2 balls of fingering (4-ply) silk/wool yarn in variegated lilac; 50g/246yd/225m

Needles:
» 4mm (US 6, UK 8) knitting needles

Size:
» Circumference: 47¼in (120cm), height: 10¾in (27cm)

Gauge (tension):
» 25 sts x 22 rows = 4in (10cm) square using 4mm (US 6, UK 8) needles over pattern

Instructions:
Cast on 68 sts then ktbl to form a neat edge.
Row 1: k2, *kfbf, k3tog, rep from * to last 2 sts, k2.
Row 2: purl.
Row 3: k2, *k3tog, kfbf, rep from * to last 2 sts, k2.
Row 4: purl.
Rep rows 1–4 until work measures approximately 47¼in (120cm).
Cast off, leaving a long yarn tail for sewing up your work.

MAKING UP
Press snood lightly. Join cast-on and cast-off edges using mattress stitch with RS facing. Weave in all loose ends.

This is a really practical snood knitted in a simple lace pattern. It is worn by twisting it round the neck twice. The mixture of silk and wool gives it a luxurious feel that makes it lovely to wear.

Bobble Scarf

Materials:
» 5 balls of bulky (chunky) yarn in grey; 50g/55–66yd/50–60m

Needles:
» 7mm (US 10½, UK 2) knitting needles

SPECIAL STITCH

MB (MAKE BOBBLE): (k1, y/o, k1, y/o, k1) into next stitch, turn and p5, turn and k1, sl1, k2tog, psso, k1, turn and p3tog. When you have made the bobble, turn and knit into the bobble st again in the main colour and then continue knitting across the row.

Instructions:
Cast on 29 sts, then ktbl to form a neat edge.

MAIN SCARF PATTERN

Row 1: knit.

Row 2 and all even rows: k7, p15, k7.

Row 3: k14, MB, k14.

Row 5: knit.

Row 7: knit.

Row 9: as row 3, MB.

Row 11: knit.

Row 12: as row 2.

Continue with this 12-row pattern ten more times and then rep rows 1–11.

Next row: as row 2.

Cast off.

MAKING UP

Weave in all loose ends.

This scarf has a really luxurious feel and will coordinate with all your winter clothes. The change of stitches adds style and the bobbles give the centre panel a focal point.

Button Cable Wrist Warmers

Materials:

» 1 ball of light worsted (DK/8-ply) merino yarn in variegated maroon; 100g/273yd/250m
» 2 red buttons

Needles:

» 4.5mm (US 7, UK 7) knitting needles
» 3.5mm (US 4, UK 9 or 10) knitting needles
» Cable needle

SPECIAL STITCHES

C6B: slip next 3 sts onto a cable needle and hold at back of work, k next 3 sts from left-hand needle, then k sts from cable needle.

C6F: slip next 3 sts onto a cable needle and hold at front of work, k the next 3 sts from left-hand needle, then k sts from cable needle.

Instructions:

Make two.

Using 3.5mm (US 4, UK 9 or 10) needles, cast on 39 sts, then ktbl to form a neat edge.

Rows 1, 3, 5 and 7: *k2, p2*, rep from * to * to last 3 sts, k2, p1.

Rows 2, 4 and 6: p1, k2, *p2, k2*, rep from * to * to end of row.

Row 8: *p4, inc1*, rep from * to * to last 3 sts, p3 (48 sts).

MAIN PATTERN

Change to 4.5mm (US 7, UK 7) needles.

Rows 1 and 5: knit.

Rows 2, 4 and 6: purl.

Row 3: C6B, C6F.

Rep the 12-stitch cable pattern three more times.

Rep rows 1–6 seven times, until work measures 6¼in (16cm).

Next row: knit.

Next row: *p6, p2tog*, rep from * to * to end of row (42 sts).

Next 6 rows: *k2, p2* rep from * to * to last 2 sts, k2.

Cast off.

MAKING UP

With RS facing, join finger end (cast-on end) 2⅜in (6cm) from the edge using mattress stitch. Join wrist end, starting from the bottom of the border section 2½in (6.5cm) down. This will leave a gap for your thumb to go through. In this cuff there is an opening at the wrist end. Sew a button at the centre of each glove on the border. Weave in all loose ends.

These cuffs are knitted in a traditional cable stitch in a variegated yarn. I have added buttons to enhance the look.

Ziggy Headband

Materials:
» 1 ball of worsted (aran/10-ply) baby alpaca/superfine merino in grey; 50g/91yd/83m
» 1 large button

Needles:
» 4.5mm (US 7, UK 7) knitting needles

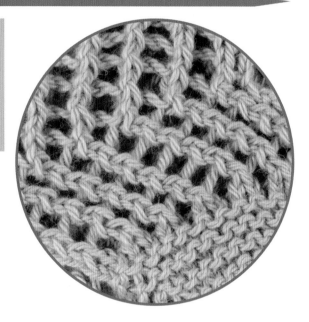

Instructions:

Cast on 8 sts, then ktbl to form a neat edge.

Rows 1–4: knit.

Rows 5, 9, 13, 17: k2, inc1, knit to last 2 sts, k1, inc1, k1.

Rows 6–8: knit.

Rows 10–12: knit.

Rows 14–16: knit.

Row 18: knit (16 sts).

RIGHT SLANT

Row 1: k1, *yo, k2tog, rep from * to last st, k1.

Row 2: purl.

Repeat these 2 rows another four times.

LEFT SLANT

Row 1: k1, *ssk, yo, rep from * to last st, k1.

Row 2: purl.

Repeat rows 1 and 2 another four times.

You will now continue to work the right-slant pattern five times then the left-slant pattern five times until work fits snugly around your head (with a slight stretch), ending with a row 10 of the left-slant pattern.

Now start decreasing as follows:

Rows 1–2: knit.

Rows 3, 7, 11: k1, k2tog, knit to last 3 sts, k2tog, k1.

Rows 4–6, 8–10, and 12: knit.

Row 13 (buttonhole row): k4, cast off 3 sts, knit to end.

Row 14: knit, casting on 3 sts over the cast-off sts.

Rows 15 and 16: knit.

Row 17: k1, k2tog, knit to last 3 sts, k2tog, k1.

Row 18: knit.

Cast off.

MAKING UP

Weave in all loose ends. Sew on button.

This is a great project to make in an evening – simply choose your favourite colour in a soft yarn.

Oakshield Boot Cuffs

Materials:

» 5 balls of super bulky (super chunky) yarn: 3 in grey (A) and 2 in turquoise (B); 100g/36yd/33m

Tools:

» 10mm (US 15, UK 000) circular knitting needle, 23½in (60cm) long
» Stitch marker

Instructions:

Make two.

Using yarn A, cast on 33 sts loosely. PM on right needle (this is to mark the beginning of the round), slip the first cast-on stitch to the left-hand needle, then knit this slipped stitch together with the last cast-on stitch. You will now have 32 sts on your needle. Slip marker as you pass it at the end of each round.

Rounds 1–12: *k1, p1* rep from * to * to end of round.

Cast off loosely, following rib pattern.

Rounds 13–15: using yarn B, knit.

Rounds 16–18: using yarn A, knit.

Rounds 19–21: using yarn B, knit.

Rounds 22–23: using yarn A, knit.

Cast off.

MAKING UP

Weave in all loose ends.

These boot cuffs will fit snugly into the top of a Wellington boot aiding warmth and comfort. The pattern can easily be adapted for a man's boots by casting on 37 sts (rather than 33 sts) and decreasing to 36 sts (rather than 32 sts). This pattern is suitable for a knitter who has mastered the basics.

Cloche Flower Hat

Materials:
- » 2 balls of fingering (4-ply) merino yarn in gooseberry (A); 50g/137yd/125m
- » Small amount of fingering (4-ply) merino yarn in grey (B)
- » A small button

Tools:
- » 3.25mm (US 3, UK 10) DPN
- » 3mm (US 2, UK 11) knitting needles
- » 3.25mm (US 3, UK 10) circular knitting needle, 16in (40cm) long
- » 3mm (US 2, UK 11) circular knitting needle, 16in (40cm) long
- » Stitch marker

Gauge (tension):
- » 23 sts x 36 rows = 4in (10cm) square using 3.25mm (US 3, UK 10) circular needle over st st

Instructions:

Using 3.25mm (UK 10, US 3) DPN and yarn A, cast on 8 sts. Divide the sts over the four needles. place a stitch marker to denote start of each round. Join the round, being careful not to twist any stitches. Slip marker as you pass it.

Round 1: kfb into each st to end of round (16 sts).

Round 2 and every even-numbered round: knit.

Round 3: *k2, yo, rep from * to end of round (24 sts).

Round 5: *k3, yo, rep from * to end of round (32 sts).

Round 7: *k4, yo, rep from * to end of round (40 sts).

Round 9: *k5, yo, rep from * to end of round (48 sts).

Continue to increase every other round (increasing 8 sts per inc round) until there are 120 sts on needles (30 sts per needle).

Transfer sts to 3.25mm (US 3, UK 10) circular needle maintaining beginning of round marker placement and place a stitch marker on this row to use for height measurement.

Work in st st (knitting every row) until work measures 3¼in (8cm) from marker.

Change to 3mm (US 2, UK 11) circular needle.

Commence 1 x 1 moss st as follows:

Round 1: *k1, p1, rep from * to end of round.

Repeat round 1 until moss st section measures 1¼in (3cm).

BRIM

Change to 3.25mm (US 3, UK 10) circular needle.

Work 2 rounds in g st (knit 1 round, purl 1 round).

Round 3: *p15, m1, rep from * to end of round (128 sts).

Round 4: purl.

Round 5: *p16, m1, rep from * to end of round (136 sts).

Round 6: purl.

Round 7: p102, turn leaving rem 34 sts unworked.

Round 8: p68, turn, leaving rem 34 sts unworked.

EAR FLAP

Round 1: p64, turn.

Round 2: p60, turn.

Continue as above, working 4 fewer sts across each round until you have 36 sts ending on a WS round.

Next round: p19, turn.

Next round: p2, turn.

Next round: p4, turn.

Next round: p6, turn.

Continue as above, working 2 more sts per round until the round p32 turn has been worked.

Next round: p35, turn.

Knit to original marker and then knit 3 rounds more.

Cast off loosely.

FLOWER

Using 3mm (US 2, UK 11) straight needles and yarn B, cast on 8 sts.

Row 1: knit tbl.

Row 2: knit.

Row 3: kfb, k to end of round (9 sts).

Row 4: knit.

Row 5: kfb, k to end of round (10 sts).

Row 6: knit.

Row 7: kfb, k to end of round (11 sts).

Row 8: knit.

Row 9: k2tog, k to end of round (10 sts).

Row 10: knit.
Row 11: k2tog, k to end of round (9 sts).
Row 12: knit.
Row 13: k2tog, k to end of round (8 sts).
Row 14: knit.
Row 15: cast off 5, knit to end of round (3 sts).
Row 16: knit 3, cast on 5 (8 sts).
Rep rows 1–16 three more times and then rows 1–14 once.
Cast off and cut yarn.

FLOWER CENTRE
Using yarn A, cast on 6 sts.
Row 1: cast off 5 sts.
Row 2: cast on 5 sts.
Repeat rows 1 and 2 seven more times.
Cast off.

MAKING UP
Join the two ends of the large flower by stitching the bottom of the end petals together. Using a running stitch run your thread along the bottom edges of the petals. Draw the stitches together to gather them up. Stitch the flower centre into the middle of the flower. Place your button in the centre of the flower and sew the complete flower onto the ear flap. Weave in all loose ends.

Harlequin Snood

Materials:
» 5 balls of light worsted (DK/8-ply) alpaca yarn: 2 in lilac (A), 1 in dark blue (B), 1 in mustard (C) and 1 in damson (D); 50g/131yd/120m

Tools:
» 4.5mm (US 7, UK 7) circular knitting needle
» Stitch marker

Size:
» Circumference: 26in (66cm), height: 15½in (39cm)

Gauge (tension):
» 21 sts x 40 rows = 4in (10cm) square using 4.5mm (US 7, UK 7) needles over pattern

Instructions:

Using yarn A, cast on 132 sts and ktbl to form a neat edge. Place a stitch marker to denote start of each round. Join the round, being careful not to twist any stitches. Slip marker as you pass it on each round.

Rounds 1–4: *k2, p2, rep from * to end of round.
Rounds 5: *k10, inc 1, rep from * to end of round (144 sts).

HONEYCOMB STITCH PATTERN
Start pattern (omitting row 1 in the first pattern repeat).
Round 1: using yarn A, knit.
Round 2: using yarn A, purl.
Rounds 3–8: using yarn B, *k4, sl2, rep from * to end of round.
Round 9: using yarn A, knit.
Round 10: using yarn A, purl.
Rounds 11–16: using yarn C, k1, *sl2, k4, rep from * to last 5 sts, sl2, k3.

Repeat the last 16 rounds using the following colour sequence for the pattern: B, C, D, noting that colour A is always used for the knit and purl rows.

Continue working the 16-round pattern repeat until the snood measures approximately 14½in (37cm).

Next round: *k10, k2tog, rep from * to end of round (132 sts).
Next round: using yarn A, purl.
Next 4 rounds: using yarn A, *k2, p2, rep from * to end of round. Cast off.

MAKING UP
Press snood lightly. Weave in all loose ends.

This snood is knitted in the round and made in a beautiful alpaca yarn where the colours blend together well.

Pompom Scarf

Materials:
» 5 balls of light worsted (DK/8-ply) yarn: 4 in sapphire (A) and 1 in cream (B); 50g/144yd/132m
» Card for pompoms

Needles:
» 5mm (US 8, UK 6) knitting needles

Instructions:
Using yarn A, cast on 42 sts, then ktbl to form a neat edge.

SCARF PATTERN
Row 1 (RS): *p3, k3*, repeat from * to * to end of row.
Row 2: knit.
Next rows: rep rows 1 and 2 until work measures 67in (170cm). Cast off.

MAKING UP
Weave in all loose ends. Make four pompoms and sew one onto each corner of your scarf using spare yarn.

This is a really simple scarf adding a twist to a basic rib. I have added contrasting pompoms for a bit of fun. As with the other scarves, the size can be altered to suit your needs.

Tiger Ruche Wrist Warmers

Materials:

» 1 ball each of fingering (4-ply) yarn in gold (A) and warm red
(B); 50g/219yd/200m

Needles:

» 3.25mm (US 3, UK 10) knitting needles

KNITTING NOTE

After the first row of the pattern you might find it helpful to knit through the back of the sts of the striped sections on the knit rows, and slip the slip sts from the back on the purl row. It will work if you do it the conventional way, but it will be a little more difficult.

Instructions:

Make two.

FRILL

Using yarn A, cast on 84 sts, then ktbl to form a neat edge.

Row 1: knit.

Row 2: purl.

Row 3: knit.

Row 4: *p2tog*, rep from * to * to end of row (42 sts).

MAIN PATTERN

Row 1: using yarn B, (k1, sl1) four times, k10, sl1, (k1, sl1) three times, k10, (k1, sl1) three times, k1.

Row 2: using yarn B, (p1, sl1) three times, p10, (p1, sl1) four times, p10, (sl1, p1) four times.

Row 3: using yarn A, sl1, (k1, sl1) three times, k11, (k1, sl1) three times, k11, (sl1, k1) three times, sl1.

Row 4: using yarn A, (sl1, p1) three times, sl1, p11, (sl1, p1) three times, p10, (p1, sl1) four times.

Repeat rows 1–4 of pattern until work measures 7½in (19cm), (20 x 4-row pattern repeats). Cut off yarn A.

Cast off with yarn B, using the picot cast-off method as follows:

Cast off 2 sts, transfer 1 st on right-hand needle to left-hand needle, *cast on 2 sts using cable cast-on, cast off 4 sts*, rep from * to * to end of row, casting off any odd stitches remaining.

MAKING UP

Join the frill at the wrist end, so that it overlaps the pattern by approximately ½in (1.5cm). Using mattress stitch, with RS facing, join the side seam 3⅜in (8.5cm) from the base of the cuff. Join the seam at the finger end, 2in (5cm) from the picot edge. This will leave a gap for your thumb. Weave in all loose ends.

These funky little cuffs are ruched to make them very feminine. I have chosen autumnal colours as I think they would look great with big woollen sweaters. The picot edging adds a certain panache.

Springtime Headband

Materials:

» 1 ball of light worsted (DK/8-ply) alpaca/merino yarn in orange;
   50g/124yd/113m

Tools:

» 4mm (US 6, UK 8) knitting needles
» Cable needle
» Stitch marker

Instructions:

Cast on 17 sts.
Work in st st until work measures 5¾in (14.5cm).

CABLE PATTERN

Rows 1, 3 and 7: p2, k6, p1, k6, p2.
Rows 2, 4, 6, 8 and all even rows: k2, p6, k1, p6, k2.
Row 5: p2, slip 3 sts onto cable needle and hold at back of work, k3,
k3 from cable needle, p1, slip 3 sts to cable needle and hold at front
of work, k3, k3 from cable needle, p2.
Rep the 8-row cable pattern until work measures 14½in (37cm),
ending on row 8 of pattern. Place a marker in the middle of the
row. Continue working in st st for another 6in (15cm) from marker.
Cast off.

MAKING UP

With RS facing, join side seams together using mattress stitch.
Weave in all loose ends.

A yarn that has some stretch is great for this
project, so that it fits snugly around your head. The
combination of stocking stitch and a cable makes
the front narrower than the sides and back.

Electric Kicks Boot Cuffs

Materials:

» 3 balls of light worsted (DK/8-ply) alpaca yarn: 2 in deep turquoise (A) and 1 in light blue (B); 50g/109yd/100m

Needles:

» 5mm (US 8, UK 6) knitting needles

Instructions:

Make two.

Using yarn A, cast on 44 sts, then ktbl to form a neat edge.

Rows 1–20: *k2, p2* rep from * to * to end of row.

PATTERN ROWS

Row 21: using yarn A (RS), knit, increasing 1 st on 22nd st (45).

Row 22: change to yarn B, purl to end of row.

Row 23: using yarn B, k1 (k1, yo, k1) into next st: *sl1, (k1, yo, k1) into next st*, rep from * to * to last st, k1.

Row 24: using yarn B, k1, k3tog tbl, *sl1, k3tog tbl*, rep from * to * to last st, k1.

Row 25: change to yarn A, knit to end of row.

Row 26: using yarn A, purl to end of row.

Row 27: change to yarn B, k2, (k1, yo, k1) into next st, *sl1, (k1, yo, k1) into next st: rep from * to * to last 2 sts, k2.

Row 28: using yarn B, p2, k3tog tbl, *sl1, k3tog tbl*, rep from * to * to last 2 sts, p2.

Rows 29–44: rep last 8 rows twice more.

Rows 45–50: rep rows 1–6 once more.

Cast off using the picot cast-off method as follows:

Cast off 2 sts, *sl remaining st on right-hand needle to left-hand needle, cast on 2 sts, cast off 4 sts*, rep from * to * to end of row.

MAKING UP

Weave in all loose ends. With RS facing, use mattress stitch to join the side seams of the pattern component of the boot cuff. Sew up the rib on the rear side of the boot cuff.

These boot cuffs have the luxurious feel of alpaca. They are the perfect finishing touch for long, elegant boots.

Autumnal Beanie

Materials:

» 2 balls of light worsted (DK/8-ply) alpaca yarn in chocolate; 50g/123yd/112m

Tools:

» 4.5mm (US 7, UK 7) circular needle, 16in (40cm) long
» 4.5mm (US 7, UK 7) DPN
» Stitch marker

Gauge (tension):

» 20 sts x 22 rows = 4in (10cm) square using 4.5mm (US 7, UK 7) needles over st st with yarn used double

Instructions:

Note: yarn is used double throughout.

Using the 4.5mm (US 7, UK 7) circular needle, cast on 80 sts. Place a stitch marker to denote the start of each round. Join the round, being careful not to twist any stitches. Slip marker as you pass it on each round.

Rounds 1–8: purl.

Rounds 9 and 10: *k1, p1, rep from * to end of round.

Work in st st (knit every round) until st st section measures 5in (12.5cm).

SHAPING CROWN

Round 1: *k8, k2tog, rep from * to end of round (72 sts).
Round 2: knit.
Round 3: *k7, k2tog, rep from * to end of round (64 sts).
Round 4: knit.
Round 5: *k6, k2tog, rep from * to end of round (56 sts).
Round 6: knit.
Round 7: *k5, k2tog, rep from * to end of round (48 sts).
Round 8: knit.

Change to DPN, distributing the sts evenly across 3 needles.

Round 9: *k4, k2tog, rep from * to end of round (40 sts).
Round 10: knit.
Round 11: *k3, k2tog, rep from * to end of round (32 sts).
Round 12: knit.
Round 13: *k2, k2tog, rep from * to end of round (24 sts).
Round 14: *k1, k2tog, rep from * to end of round (16 sts).

MAKING UP

Cut yarn and thread through remaining stitches. Pull yarn up tightly and fasten off. Weave in all loose ends. If you weave your ends in neatly, the hat can also be worn with the purl side out for a slightly different look.

Starry Night Snood

Materials:
» 3 balls of light worsted (DK/8-ply) silk yarn in variegated blue-green; 100g/153yd/140m

Needles:
» 5mm (US 8, UK 6) knitting needles
» Cable needle

Size:
» Circumference: 50½in (128cm), height: 9in (23cm)

Gauge (tension):
» 19 sts x 22 rows = 4in (10cm) square using 5mm (US 8, UK 6) needles over pattern

Instructions:

Cast on 44 sts, then ktbl to form a neat edge.

Row 1: k11, p3, k2, p4, k4, p4, k2, p3, k11.

Row 2 and all even-numbered rows: k11, work each of the next 22 ksts as it appears on this side of the work (knit the k sts and purl the p sts), k11.

Row 3: k11, p3, k2, p4, C4B, p4, k2, p3, k11.

Row 5: k11, p3, T3F, p2, T3B, T3F, p2, T3B, p3, k11.

Row 7: k11, p4, T3F, T3B, p2, T3F, T3B, p4, k11.

Row 9: k11, p5, C4B, p4, C4B, p5, k11.

Row 11: k11, p5, k4, p4, k4, p5, k11.

Row 13: as row 9.

Row 15: k11, p4, T3B, T3F, p2, T3B, T3F, p4, k11.

Row 17: k11, p3, T3B, p2, T3F, T3B, p2, T3F, p3, k11.

Row 19: as row 3.

Rep rows 1–20 until work measures approximately 50½in (128cm). Cast off, leaving a long yarn tail for sewing up your work.

MAKING UP

Press snood lightly. Join cast-on and cast-off ends using mattress stitch with RS facing. Weave in all loose ends.

This snood is made from a hand-dyed silk that gives it a wonderful rich colour and sheen, highlighted by the raised cable pattern. The snood can be worn by wrapping it round the neck twice.

Zebra Razzle Scarf

Materials:
» 2 balls each of light worsted (DK/8-ply) yarn in black (A) and cream (B); 50g/144yd/132m

Needles:
» 4.5mm (US 7, UK 7) knitting needles
» 4mm (US 6, UK 8) knitting needles

Instructions:

Using 4mm (US 6, UK 8) needles and yarn A, cast on 49 sts, then ktbl to form a neat edge.

RIB SECTION
Row 1: *k1, p1*, repeat from * to * to last st, k1.
Row 2: *p1, k1*, repeat from * to * to last st, p1.
Rows 3 and 4: rep rows 1 and 2.

STRIPE PATTERN SECTION
Change to 4.5mm (US 7, UK 7) needles.
Row 1: to set the pattern, purl 1 row in yarn A.
Row 2 (RS): using yarn B, (k1, sl1) five times, *k10, sl1, (k1, sl1) four times*, rep from * to * once more to last st, k1.
Row 3: using yarn B, (p1, sl1) five times, *p10, sl1 (p1, sl1) four times*, rep from * to * once more to last st, p1.
Row 4: using yarn A, k2, sl1, (k1, sl1) three times, *k12, sl1, (k1, sl1) three times*, rep * to * once more to last 2 sts, k2.
Row 5: using yarn A, p2, sl1, (p1, sl1) three times, *p12, sl1, (p1, sl1) three times*, rep * to * once more to last 2 sts, p2.
Next rows: continue in set pattern (rows 2–5 only) until work measures approximately 62¼in (158cm), ending with a row 5. Cut off yarn B.
Next row: change to size 4mm (US 6, UK 8) needles and knit using yarn A.
Next 4 rows: work rows 1–4 of the rib section as you did at the start of the scarf.
Cast off.

MAKING UP
Weave in all loose ends.

This funky little scarf cleverly ruches in panels. I have made it in traditional black and white using ultra-soft alpaca yarn.

Autumn Wrist Warmers

Materials:

» 1 ball each of light worsted (DK/8-ply) yarn in grey (A), wine (B), mustard (C) and moss (D); 50g/131yd/120m

Needles:

» 4mm (US 6, UK 8) knitting needles
» 4.5mm (US 7, UK 7) knitting needles

Instructions:

Make two. Using 4mm (US 6, UK 8) needles and yarn A, cast on 40 sts, then ktbl to form a neat edge.

Rows 1 and 2: *k1, p1*, rep from * to * to end of row.

Change to 4.5mm (US 7, UK 7) needles.

Row 3: *k2B, k2C*, rep from * to * to end of row.

Rows 4–7: using yarn D, st st starting with a purl row. Cut off yarn D.

Row 8: *p2C, p2B*, rep from * to * to end of row.

Rows 9–12: using yarn A, st st.

Rep rows 3–12 three more times and then rows 3–8 once more.

BORDER AT THE FINGER END

Change to size 4mm (US 6, UK 8) needles and, using yarn A, work 2 rows in k1, p1 rib.

Cast off.

MAKING UP

With RS facing, join the side seam 3 1/8in (8cm) from the wrist end and 2 3/8in (6cm) from the finger end, using mattress stitch. This will leave a gap for your thumb to go through. Weave in all loose ends.

These cuffs are very simple to make and I have used muted colours that blend in well together. Use the pattern to make a matching scarf to add style to your winter wardrobe.

Flossie Flower Headband

Materials:

» 1 ball each of light worsted (DK/8-ply) alpaca/merino yarn in pink, cream and orange; 50g/124yd/113m
» 5 small, ready-made pompoms for the flower centres
» A length of stretchy jersey as the base for the headband, approximately 30in (76cm) long for a child/young adult's head, plus extra for tying; alternatively, use a ready-made headband

Needles:

» 4mm (US 6, UK 8) knitting needles

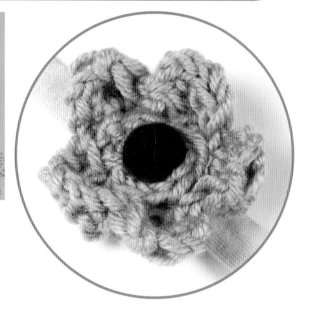

Instructions:

FLOWERS

Make five. Using colour of your choice, cast on 4 sts.

Row 1: k4.

Row 2: in the first st (k1, p1, k1tbl, p1, k1tbl), turn, k5, turn, p5, turn, k5, turn, p2tog twice, p1. Place the yarn to the back of your work, slip the second and third sts over the first stitch.

Row 3: purl 3 remaining sts on left-hand needle.

Rep rows 1–3 three times and then rows 1 and 2 once more. Cast off remaining sts purlwise.

MAKING UP

Weave in all loose ends. Sew the cast-on edge and cast-off edge of each flower together. Sew one pompom in the centre of each flower. Sew one flower in the centre of the length of jersey and space the other four 2¼in (6cm) apart across the front of the band. The two ends can be knotted together once the band is on your head.

This headband is reminiscent of spring flowers and bursts of colour after the winter months, and the flowers are quick and easy to make. The finished headband will fit a teenager or young adult, and can be easily adapted to fit any size.

Jester Boot Cuffs

Materials:
» 5 balls of light worsted (DK/8-ply) pure alpaca yarn: 2 in red (A) and 1 each in gold (B), green (C) and black (D); 50g/109yd/100m

Needles:
» 5mm (US 8, UK 6) knitting needles

SPECIAL STITCH
MB (MAKE BOBBLE): (k1, yo, k1, yo, k1) into next stitch, turn and p5, turn and k1, sl1, k2tog, psso, k1, turn and p3tog. Cut off yarn and thread it through st rem on needle. Sew end into bobble to make it rounded. .

Instructions:

Make two.

Using yarn A, cast on 1 st.

Row 1: knit.

Using cable cast on, cast on first on each side of every alternate row (odd row numbers) until you have 15 sts on your needle. Knit every even row.

Cut off yarn after 14th row. Continue to make three more triangles in the same way, using yarns B, C and D. Leave all of your triangles on one needle.

MAIN BODY
Using yarn D with wrong side facing, purl across all four triangles increasing 1st in between each triangle and one more increase at the end (64 sts).

Next 4 rows: st st. Change to yarn C.

Next 6 rows: st st. Change to yarn B.

Next 6 rows: st st. Change to yarn A.

Next 6 rows: st st.

RIBBED TOP
Rows 1–19: using yarn A, *k2, p2* rep from * to * to end of row. Cast off.

MAKING UP
Weave in all loose ends. With RS facing, use mattress stitch to join the side seams of the pattern component of the boot cuff. Sew up the rib on the rear side of the boot cuff. Make one bobble in each colour of yarn. Sew bobbles onto points at the bottom of your boot cuff as follows: yarn A bobble onto yarn C point; yarn B bobble onto yarn D point; yarn C bobble onto yarn A point and yarn D bobble onto yarn B point.

The pointed, bobbly edges add a festival feel to these boot cuffs and they will fit Wellington boots with ease, preventing them from chafing bare summer legs. This pattern is suitable for a knitter with some experience.

Fair Isle Beanie

Materials:
» 1 ball each of fingering (4-ply) baby alpaca/silk yarn in navy (A), cream (B), coral (C) and mid blue (D); 50g/246yd/225m

Tools:
» 3.25mm (US 3, UK 10) circular knitting needle, 16in (40cm)
» 3.25mm (US 3, UK 10) DPN
» Stitch marker

Gauge (tension):
» 32 sts x 35 rows = 4in (10cm) using 3.25mm (US 3, UK 10) circular needle over Fair Isle pattern

Instructions:

Using the circular needle and yarn A, cast on 128 sts. Place a stitch marker to denote start of each round. Join the round, being careful not to twist any stitches. Slip marker as you pass it on each round.

Rounds 1–8: using yarn A, *k1, p1, rep from * to end of round.

Next round: *k3, inc in next stitch, rep from * to end of round (160 sts).

Next 3 rounds: work from chart A.

Chart A

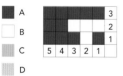

Next round: using yarn A, *k9, kfb in next stitch, rep from * to end of round (176 sts).

Next 13 rounds: work from chart B.

Chart B

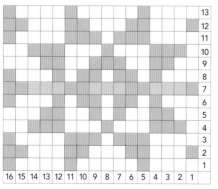

Next round: using yarn A, *k10 inc in next stitch, rep from * to end of round (192 sts).

Next round: using yarn B, increase 3 sts evenly across round (195 sts).

Next 9 rounds: work from chart C.

Chart C

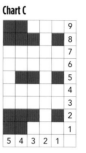

Next round: using yarn B, decrease 3 stitches evenly across the row (192 sts).

Next round: using yarn A, *k4, k2tog, rep from * to end of round (160 sts).

Next 9 rounds: work from chart D.

Chart D

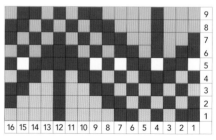

Next round: using yarn A, *k3, k2tog, rep from * to end of round (128 sts).

Next 4 rounds: work from chart E. Note that for the last 3 sts, you knit the first 3 sts from the chart.

Chart E

Now distribute your stitches evenly across 4 DPN.

Next round: k4, *k2, k2tog, rep from * to last 4 sts, k4 (98 sts).

Next 3 rounds: work as rounds 4–6 from chart C, reversing colours and noting the round finishes on the first stitch from the chart. On the third round inc 2 sts (100 sts).

Work 4 rounds from chart F; when you reach xxx work sl1, k2tog, psso over those 3 sts (90 sts).

Chart F

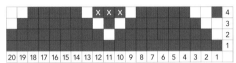

Next 2 rounds: work from chart G decreasing as above for xxx (80 sts).

Chart G

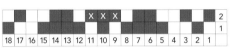

Next round: knit using yarn A.

Next round: *k7, sl 1, k2tog, psso, k6, rep from * to end of round (70 sts).

Next round: *k4D, k3C, rep from * to end of round.

Next round: *k4D, k3C, sl1, k2tog, psso, k1 (all D), k3C, rep from * to end of round (60 sts).

Next round: knit each stitch as it appears in the same colours as the previous row.

Next round: using yarn B, *k4, sl1, k2tog, psso, k5, rep from * to end of round (50 sts).

Next round: using yarn B, knit.

Next round: using yarn B, *k3, sl1, k2tog, psso, k4, rep from * to end of round (40 sts).

Next round: using yarn B, *k2, sl1, k2tog, psso, k3, rep from * to end of round (30 sts).

Next round: *sl1, k2tog, psso, rep from * to end of round (10 sts).

MAKING UP

Cut yarn and thread through rem sts. Pull yarn up tightly and fasten off. Weave in all loose ends.

Caramel Snood

Materials:
» 3 balls of light worsted (DK/8-ply) baby alpaca/superfine merino yarn in butterscotch; 50g/122yd/112m

Needles:
» 4.5mm (US 7, UK 7) circular knitting needle
» Stitch marker

Size:
» Circumference: 47in (119cm), height: 8in (20cm)

Gauge (tension):
» 15 sts x 29 rows = 4in (10cm) square using 4.5mm (US 7, UK 7) circular needle over pattern

Instructions:
Cast on 181 sts. Place a stitch marker to denote start of each round. Join the round, being careful not to twist any stitches. Slip marker as you pass it on each round.

Round 1: k1, *yo, k2tog, rep from * to end of round.

Rounds 2 and 3: knit.

Repeat the above 3 rounds until work measures approximately 8in (20cm) in height.

Cast off.

MAKING UP
Press snood lightly. Weave in all loose ends.

This is a really simple snood for a beginner who has mastered the basics. It is knitted in the round and will wrap round the neck twice. The luxury yarn makes it lovely and soft next to the skin.

Bolero Scarf

Materials:
- 4 balls of super bulky (super chunky) yarn in turquoise; 100g/35yd/32m
- Card for pompoms

Needles:
- 9mm (US 13, UK 00) knitting needles

Instructions:

SCARF SECTION 1
Cast on 3 sts.
Row 1: knit.
Row 2: k1, m1, k1, m1, k1.
Row 3: knit.
Row 4: k1, m1, k3, m1, k1.
Row 5: knit.
Row 6: k1, m1, k5, m1, k1.
Row 7: knit.
Row 8: k1, m1, k7, m1, k1.
Row 9: knit.
Row 10: k1, m1, k9, m1, k1.
Row 11: knit.
Row 12: k1, m1, k11, m1, k1.
Row 13: knit.
Row 14: purl.
Rows 15–20: rep rows 13 and 14 three more times.
Rows 21 and 22: knit.

SCARF SECTION 2
Rows 1–8: work st st.
Rows 9 and 10: knit.
Rep rows 1–10 until work measures 49¼in (125cm), ending with 2 knit rows.

DECREASING ROWS
Odd-numbered rows: k2tog, knit to last 2 sts, k2tog.
Even-numbered rows: knit.
Continue knitting until there are 3 sts left, ending with an even-numbered row.
Cast off.

MAKING UP
Make two pompoms from turquoise yarn using 2in (5cm) cardboard circles with 1in (2.5cm) holes in the centre. Weave in all loose ends. Using the yarn from the pompoms, attach one to the cast-on edge and one to the decreased edge of your scarf.

This is an extremely simple scarf that will keep you very cosy on a winter's day. It can be knitted over an evening or two.

Pastel Wrist Warmers

Materials:
» 1 ball each of light worsted (DK/8-ply) alpaca yarn in cream (A), rose pink (B) and sandstone (C); 50g/131yd/120m

Needles:
» 4mm (US 6, UK 8) knitting needles

Instructions:

RIGHT HAND
Using yarn A, cast on 40 sts, then ktbl to form a neat edge.
Row 1 (RS): *k1, p1* rep from * to * to end of row.
Row 2: *p1, k1* rep from * to * to end of row.
Work 8 more rows in rib, ending with a WS row.

SHAPING FOR THUMB
Rows 11 and 12: using yarn B, st st.
Row 13: using yarn B, k20, m1, k5, m1, k15 (42 sts).
Row 14: using yarn B, purl.
Rows 15 and 16: using yarn C, st st.
Row 17: k20, m1, k7, m1, k15 (at the same time incorporating pattern), k1C, *k3A, k3C* rep from * to * until last stitch, k1A (44 sts).
Row 18: p1C, *p1A, p1C, p1A, p1C, p1B, p1C* rep from * to * to last st, k1A.
Row 19: as row 17, following the stitch sequence without the increase.
Row 20: using yarn C, purl.
Row 21: using yarn C, k20, m1, k9, m1, k15 (46 sts). Cut off yarn C.
Rows 22–24: using yarn B, st st, starting with a purl row.
Row 25: using yarn B, k20, m1, k11, m1, k15 (48 sts).
Row 26: using yarn A, purl.
Rows 27 and 28: using yarn A, st st.

DIVIDE FOR THUMB
Next row (RS): using yarn A, k33, turn.
Next row: using yarn C, p13. Continue working on these 13 sts only.
Row 1: using yarn C, knit.

Row 2: p3C, p3A, p3C, p3A, p1C.
Row 3: *k1A, k1C, k1B, k1C, k1A, k1C* rep from * to * once more, then k1A.
Row 4: as row 2.
Rows 5 and 6: using yarn C, st st. Cut off yarn C.
Row 7: using yarn A, knit.
Row 8: using yarn A, purl.
Sew side seam of thumb together.
Now rejoin yarn A. With RS facing, pick up two stitches from the base of the thumb, then knit to end of row (37 sts).
Next row: using yarn C, purl.
Work st st over the next 13 rows in colours/pattern as follows:
Row 1: using yarn C, knit.
Row 2: *p3A, p3C* rep from * to * to last st, p1A.
Row 3: k1C, *k1A, k1C, k1A, k1C, k1B, k1C* rep from * to * to end of row.
Row 4: as row 2.
Rows 5 and 6: using yarn C, st st.
Rows 7–10: using yarn A, st st. Cut off yarn A.
Rows 11–14: using yarn B, st st.
Row 15: using yarn C, *k1, p1*, rep from * to * to last st, k1.
Row 16: using yarn C, *p1, k1*, rep from * to * to last st, p1.
Cast off.

LEFT HAND

Work as for right hand up to the thumb shaping.

Rows 11 and 12: using yarn B, st st.

Row 13: using yarn B, k15, m1, k5, m1, k20 (42 sts).

Row 14: using yarn B, purl.

Rows 15 and 16: using yarn C, st st.

Row 17: k15, m1, k7, m1, k20 (at the same time incorporating pattern), k1C, *k3A, k3C*, rep from * to * to last stitch, k1A (44 sts).

Row 18: p1C, *p1A, p1C, p1A, p1C, p1B, p1C*, rep from * to * to last st, p1A.

Row 19: as row 17, following the stitch sequence without the increase.

Row 20: using yarn C, purl.

Row 21: using yarn C, k15, m1, k9, m1, k20 (46 sts). Cut off yarn C.

Rows 22–24: using yarn B, st st, starting with a purl row.

Row 25: using yarn B, k15, m1, k11, m1, k20 (48 sts).

Row 26: using yarn A, purl.

Rows 27 and 28: using yarn A, st st.

DIVIDE FOR THUMB

Next row (RS): using yarn A, k33, turn.

Next row: using yarn C, p13. Now continue working on these 13 sts only. Work the thumb as for the right hand.

Continue working the pattern as for the right hand until the wrist cuff is complete.

MAKING UP

With RS facing, sew up the side seam using mattress stitch. Weave in all loose ends.

These wrist cuffs are made with a luxury alpaca in pastel colours and have a hint of Fair Isle in them.

Red Robin Headband

Materials:

» 1 ball of worsted (aran/10-ply) Bluefaced Leicester yarn in red; 50g/91yd/83m

Needles:

» 5mm (US 8, UK 6) knitting needles
» Cable needle

Instructions:

Cast on 87 sts, then ktbl to form a neat edge.

Row 1: k1, p2tog, *k1, p1, rep from * to last 3 sts, p2tog, k1 (85 sts).

Row 2: *k1, p1, rep from * to end of row.

Insert pattern as follows (the pattern is repeated five times across each row as a 17-st pattern repeat):

Row 1 (RS): *p6, k2tog, yfrn, p1, yo, sl1, k1, psso, p6, rep from * to end of row.

Row 2: *k6, p1, k3, p1, k6, rep from * to end of row.

Row 3: *p5, k2tog, yfrn, p3, yo, sl1, k1, psso, p5, rep from * to end of row.

Row 4: *(k5, p1) twice, k5, rep from * to end of row.

Row 5: *p4, k2tog, yfrn, (p1, k1) twice, p1, yo, sl1, k1, psso, p4, rep from * to end of row.

Row 6: *k4, p1, k2, p1, k1, p1, k2, p1, k4, rep from * to end of row.

Row 7: *p3, k2tog, yfrn, p2, k1, p1, k1, p2, yo, sl1, k1, psso, p3, rep from * to end of row.

Row 8: *(k3, p1) twice, k1, (p1, k3) twice, rep from * to end of row.

Row 9: *p2, k2tog, yfrn, p2, k2tog, yfrn, p1, yo, sl1, k1, psso, p2, yo, sl1, k1, psso, p2, rep from * to end of row.

Row 10: *k2, (p1, k3) three times, p1, k2, rep from * to end of row.

Row 11 (bobble row): *p2, (k1, p1, k1, p1) into next st, turn, p4, turn, k4, turn, p4, turn, sl1, k1, psso, k2tog, turn, p2tog, turn, slip bobble onto right-hand needle (bobble completed), p2, k2tog, yfrn, p3, yo, sl1, k1, psso, p2, make second bobble and slip it onto right-hand needle, p2, rep from * to end of row.

Row 12: as row 4.

Row 13: k1, p2tog, *k1, p1, rep from * to last 3 sts, k2tog, p1 (83 sts).

Row 14: *k1, p1, rep from * to end of row.

Cast off.

MAKING UP

With RS facing, join seams together using mattress stitch. Weave in all loose ends.

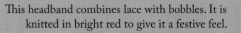

This headband combines lace with bobbles. It is knitted in bright red to give it a festive feel.

Art Deco Boot Cuffs

Materials:
» 1 ball each of worsted (aran/10-ply) textured yarn in mustard (A) and green (B), and a small amount in brown (C); 100g/138yd/125m

Needles:
» 5mm (US 8, UK 6) knitting needles
» 6mm (US 10, UK 4) knitting needles

KNITTING NOTE
Cut yarn C into small lengths to make working with three colours more manageable.

Instructions:

Make two.

Using 5mm (US 8, UK 6) needles and yarn A, cast on 54 sts.

Row 1: *k2, p2* rep to last 2 sts, k2.

Row 2: *p2, k2* rep to last 2 sts, p2.

Rows 19–21: rep the last 2 rows nine more times and then row 1 once more.

Row 22: p1, inc 1 into next st, continue in rib until 54th st, inc 1, p last sts. You will now have 56 sts on your needle.

Change to 6mm (US 10, UK 4) needles and work 14 rows from the chart.

Work the pattern from stitch 1–26, then rep the whole chart once more.

Work sts 3–6 once more (this ensures you do not end up with a thick green seam).

Cut off yarns A and C.

Rib rows 1 and 2: *k2, p2* rep from * to * to end of row. Cast off.

MAKING UP
Weave in all loose ends. With RS facing, use mattress stitch to join the side seams of the pattern component of the boot cuff. Sew up the rib on the rear side of the boot cuff.

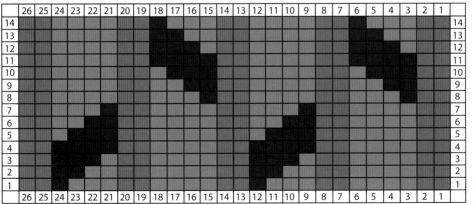

| A | B | C |

The pattern for these elegant boot cuffs is suitable for an experienced knitter. The autumnal colours complement long brown boots very well.

Lacy Rose Beret

Materials:
» 1 ball of light worsted (DK/8-ply) yarn in pale pink; 50g/191yd/175m
» 1 button (optional)

Tools:
» 3.75mm (US 5, UK 9) knitting needles
» 4.5mm (US 7, UK 7) circular needle, 16in (40cm) long
» 4.5mm (US 7, UK 7) DPN
» Cable needle
» Stitch marker

Gauge (tension):
» 18 sts x 30 rows = 4in (10cm) square using 4.5mm (US 7, UK 7) needles over lace pattern

Instructions:

Please check tension carefully before starting the hat.
Using 3.75mm (US 5, UK 9) needles, cast on 118 sts.
Row 1 (RS): *k2, C4F, rep from * to last 4 sts, k4.
Row 2: purl.
Row 3: knit.
Row 4: purl.
Rows 5 and 6: as rows 1 and 2.
Row 7: *C4B, k2 rep from * to last 4 sts, C4B.
Row 8: purl.
Knit sts onto a 4.5mm (US 7, UK 7) circular needle increasing 2 sts evenly across the row (120 sts).
Join to work in the round and place a stitch marker to denote start of each round. Slip marker as you pass it on each round.
Round 1: *k4, yo, k1, sl 1, k1, psso k3, rep from * to end of round.
Round 2: *k2, k2togtbl, k1, yo, k5, rep from * to end of round.
Round 3: *k6, yo, k1, sl 1, k1, psso, k1, rep from * to end of round.
Round 4: *k2togtbl, k1, yo, k7, rep from * to end of round.
Round 5: *k3, k2tog, k1, yo, k4, rep from * to end of round.
Round 6: *k5, yo, k1, k2tog, k2, rep from * to end of round.
Round 7: *k1, k2tog, k1, yo, k6, rep from * to end of round.

Round 8: *k7, yo, k1, k2tog, rep from * to end of round.
Repeat rows 1–8 twice more and then rows 1–4 once more.

DECREASING FOR CROWN
Change to DPN when yarn becomes tight on circular needles.
Round 1: *k5, sk2po (sl1t, k2tog, psso), k4, rep from * to end of round (100 sts).
Round 2: knit.
Round 3: *k4, sk2po, k3, rep from * to end of round (80 sts).
Round 4: knit.
Round 5: *k3, sk2po, k2, rep from * to end of round (60 sts).
Round 6: *k2, sk2po, k1, rep from * to end of round (40 sts).
Round 7: *k1, sk2po, rep from * to end of round (20 sts).
Round 8: *k1, sk2po, k1, rep from * to end of round (16 sts).
Cut yarn, leaving a long tail.

MAKING UP
Pull yarn up tightly and fasten off securely. Join border seam using mattress stitch. Sew a button onto where the seams are joined at the bottom of the hat if you wish.

Matisse Snood

Materials:
» 4 balls of light worsted (DK/8-ply) alpaca yarn: 3 in dark grey (A) and 1 in mustard (B); 50g/131yd/120m

Needles:
» 4mm (US 6, UK 8) knitting needles

Size:
» Circumference: 29½in (75cm), height: 12¼in (31cm)

Gauge (tension):
» 19 sts x 26 rows = 4in (10cm) square using 4mm (US 6, UK 8) needles over pattern

Instructions:

Using yarn A, cast on 64 sts, then ktbl to form a neat edge.

Row 1 (RS): knit.

Row 2: k3, purl to last 3 sts, k3.

Continue this 2-row pattern until work measures 29½in (75cm) ending with a WS row.

Fasten off yarn A.

Using yarn B, work picot method cast-off as follows:

Next row: k2, cast off 2 sts, *transfer st on right-hand needle to left-hand needle and cast on 2 sts using cable cast-on, cast off 4 sts, repeat from * to end of row.

MAKING UP

Press snood lightly. Join ends using yarn B, slightly gathering the picot edge so it matches the cast-on edge. Weave in all loose ends.

This is a very simple snood that is quick to knit. It has a stylish edge in a contrasting colour that gives it a certain panache.

Simple Lace Scarf

Materials:
» 2 balls of light worsted (DK/8-ply) silk blend yarn in variegated green-blue, 100g/295yd/270m

Needles:
» 4.5mm (US 7, UK 7) knitting needles

Instructions:

Cast on 47 sts in variegated green-blue, then ktbl to form a neat edge.

SCARF PATTERN

Row 1 (RS): knit.

Row 2: purl.

Row 3 (RS): k2, *yfwd, k2tog, k1*, repeat from * to * to end of row.

Row 4: purl.

Rep rows 1–4 until work measures 71½in (182cm).

Cast off.

MAKING UP

Weave in all loose ends.

This scarf will suit all seasons as it is made from a mixture of merino wool and silk. It is made from a very simple lace stitch and the length and width can be adapted to suit your taste.

Breakfast at Tiffany's Wrist Warmers

Materials:
» 1 ball each of light worsted (DK/8-ply) yarn in blue (A) and lilac (B); 50g/131yd/120m

Needles:
» 4mm (US 6, UK 8) knitting needles
» 3.75mm (US 5, UK 9) knitting needles

SPECIAL STITCH
MB (MAKE BOBBLE): All three sts are made from the same st.
Row 1: knit into the front, back and front again of the same st.
Row 2: p3, turn.
Row 3: sl1, k1, psso, k1, turn.
Row 4: p2tog, turn.

Instructions:

RIGHT HAND
Start at the border (finger end).
Using 3.75mm (US 5, UK 9) needles and yarn A, cast on 40 sts, then ktbl to form a neat edge.
Rows 1–4: *k1, p1*, rep from * to * to end of row.
Change to 4mm (US 6, UK 8) needles and start pattern as follows, decreasing 1 st on first row only (40 sts).
Row 1: (k2, p2) three times, MB using yarn B, knit same st again using yarn A, k1, p2, *k2, p2*, rep from * to * to end of row.
Rows 2, 4 and 6: *p2, k2*, rep from * to * to end of row.
Row 3: *k2, p2*, rep from * to * to end of row.
Row 5: as row 3.
Repeat the above 6 rows nine more times. Cut off yarn A and change to 3.75mm (US 5, UK 9) needles and yarn B.
Next row: *k1, k2tog, k9, k2tog*, rep from * to * twice, then k12.
Next two rows: *k1, p1*, rep from * to * to end of row.

Cast off using small picot cast-off as follows:
k2, cast off 1 st, *transfer st on right-hand needle to left-hand needle and cast on 1 st using cable cast-on, cast off 2 sts*, rep from * to * to end of row.

LEFT HAND
As right hand until start of pattern (where you change to 4mm (US 6, UK 8) needles), then place bobbles as follows:
Row 1: *k2, p2*, rep from * to * seven times, MB, (k2, p2) three times.
Continue with above spacing for bobbles using the same row sequence as right wrist warmer.

MAKING UP
Using mattress stitch, join side seam 2¼in (5.5cm) from the finger end and 3¼in (8.5cm) from picot edge. This will leave a gap for your thumb to go through. Weave in all loose ends.

These handwarmers remind me of the film *Breakfast at Tiffany's*. They are elegant and warm, and can be knitted in colours of your choice.

Dynamic Wave Headband

Materials:
» 1 ball each of light worsted (DK/8-ply) alpaca/merino yarn in grey (A) and dusky pink (B); 50g/124yd/113m

Needles:
» 4mm (US 6, UK 8) knitting needles

KNITTING NOTE
When working from the chart, please note that the knit rows are the odd-numbered rows and the purl rows are the even-numbered rows. Remember to twist yarn every 3–4 sts to avoid large loops forming at the back of your work.

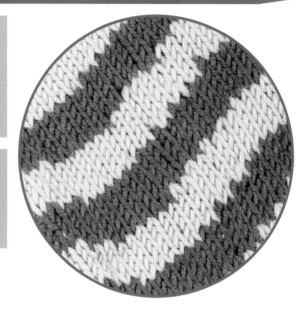

Instructions:
Using yarn A, cast on 28 sts and ktbl to form a neat edge.
Join yarn B and continue by working the 10-row pattern from the chart below until work measures approximately 18in (46cm). This allows for some 'give' when placed around an adult's head.
Fasten off yarn B.
Knit 1 row in yarn A.
Cast off.

MAKING UP
With RS facing, join side seams together using mattress stitch.
Weave in all loose ends.

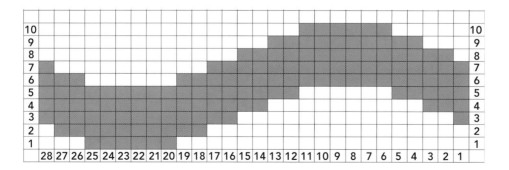

This is a great headband for all ages.
Simply choose your favourite colours
to match your outfit.

Button Boot Cuffs

Materials:

» 1 ball of worsted (aran/10-ply) textured yarn in mid blue; 100g/138yd/125m

» 4 large wooden buttons

Needles:

» 5.5mm (US 9, UK 5) knitting needles

Instructions:

Make two.

Cast on 54 sts and ktbl to form a neat edge.

Row 1: knit into the back of sts to form a neat edge.

Row 2: *k2, p2* rep to last 2 sts, k2.

Row 3: *p2, k2* rep to last 2 sts, p2.

Row 4: as row 2.

Row 5: as row 3.

Rows 6–23: rep rows 2–5 four more times and then rows 2 and 3 once more.

Row 24: cast off 6 sts then *k1, p1* to end of row.

Rows 25–39: *p1, k1*, rep from * to * to end of row.

Row 40: cast off, leaving a long piece of yarn to sew up seams.

MAKING UP

With RS facing, use mattress stitch to join the side seams of the rib component of the boot cuff. Turn the boot cuff inside out and sew the cast-off flap onto the main body of the cuff with a neat hemming stitch. Sew up the flap on the reverse side. Weave in all loose ends. Using mid blue yarn, sew one button at the top edge of the flap and one at the bottom edge of the flap.

The blue wool and decorative wooden buttons look great with jeans and will fit any wide-topped boot. The colour can easily be changed to suit your wardrobe. The pattern is a double moss stitch and is suitable for a knitter who has mastered the basics.

Chunky-knit Beanie

Materials:
» 1 ball of worsted (aran/10-ply) yarn in teal; 100g/126yd/115m

Needles:
» 6mm (US 10, UK 4) knitting needles
» 1 cable needle

Gauge (tension):
» over moss stitch: 16 sts x 20 rows = 4in (10cm) square using 6mm (US 10, UK 4) needles
» over double moss stitch: 14 sts x 20 rows = 4in (10cm) square using 6mm (US 10, UK 4) needles

Instructions:

Note: pattern uses moss stitch and double moss stitch.

CABLE BAND

Cast on 16 sts, then ktbl to form a neat edge.

Row 1 (RS): knit.

Row 2: purl.

Rows 3 and 4: as rows 1 and 2.

Row 5: C14B, k2.

Row 6: purl.

Rows 7 and 8: as rows 1 and 2.

These 8 rows form the pattern for the band.

Rep rows 1–8 until band measures approximately 23½in (60cm), ending with row 8.

Cast off, leaving last st on your needle.

MAIN BODY

With RS facing, pick up and knit 75 sts along the straight edge of the cable band.

Row 1 (WS): *k2, p2, rep from * to last 3 sts, k2, p1.

Row 2 (RS): p1, k2, *p2, k2, rep from * to end.

Continue working in double moss stitch until work measures approximately 5in (13cm) with RS facing for next row.

Now work in single moss stitch and at the same time decrease for the crown as follows:

Row 1: *moss st 6, work 3 tog, moss st 6, rep from * to end of row (65 sts).

Rows 2–4: work 3 rows single moss st.

Row 5: *moss st 5, work 3 tog, moss st 5, rep from * to end of row (55 sts).

Row 6 and all even-numbered rows to row 14: single moss st.

Row 7: *moss st 4, work 3 tog, moss st 4, rep from * to end of row (45 sts).

Row 9: *moss st 3, work 3 tog, moss st 3, rep from * to end of row (35 sts).

Row 11: *moss st 2, work 3 tog, moss st 2, rep from * to end of row (25 sts).

Row 13: *moss st 1, work 3 tog, moss st 1, rep from * to end of row (15 sts).

Row 15: *work 3 sts tog, rep from * to end of row.

MAKING UP

Cut yarn and thread through remaining stitches. Pull yarn up tightly and fasten off securely. Join back seam using mattress stitch.

Muriel Snood

Materials:
» 3 balls of light worsted (DK/8-ply) silk/merino yarn in variegated pink-orange; 50g/135yd/150m

Needles:
» 4mm (US 6, UK 8) knitting needles

Size:
» Circumference: 47in (119cm), height: 8½in (21cm)

Gauge (tension):
» 22 sts x 30 rows = 4in (10cm) square using 4mm (US 6, UK 8) needles over pattern

Instructions:

Cast on 56 sts.

Row 1 (RS): k5, p to last 5 sts, k5.

Row 2: knit.

Row 3: k5, *p2, (k2, p2) twice, k8, rep from * once more, p2, (k2, p2) twice, k5.

Row 4: k5, *k2, (p2, k2) twice, p8, rep from * once more, k2, (p2, k2) twice, k5.

Row 5: as row 1.

Row 6: as row 2.

Row 7: as row 3.

Row 8: as row 4.

Row 9: as row 3.

Row 10: as row 4.

Row 11: k5, *p2, T3F, T3B, p2, k8, rep from * once more, p2, T3F, T3B, p2, k5.

Row 12: k5, *k3, p4, k3, p8, rep from * once more, k3, p4, k3, k5.

Row 13: k5, *p3, C4B, p3, k8, rep from * once more, p3, C4B, p3, k5.

Row 14: as row 12.

Row 15: k5, *p2, T3B, T3F, p2, k8, rep from * once more, p2, T3B, T3F, p2, k5.

Row 16: as row 4.

Row 17: as row 3.

Row 18: as row 4.

Rep the 18-row pattern another nineteen times or until work measures approximately 47in (119cm).

Cast off loosely, leaving a long yarn tail for sewing up your work.

MAKING UP

Press snood lightly. Join cast-on and cast-off ends using mattress stitch with RS facing. Weave in all loose ends.

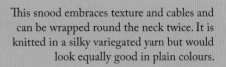

This snood embraces texture and cables and can be wrapped round the neck twice. It is knitted in a silky variegated yarn but would look equally good in plain colours.

Caramel Wrist Warmers

Materials:

» 1 ball each of light worsted (DK/8-ply) alpaca/baby merino yarn in butterscotch (A) and ivory (B); 50g/122yd/112m

Needles:

» 4mm (US 6, UK 8) knitting needles
» 4.5mm (US 7, UK 7) knitting needles

Instructions:

Make two. Using 4mm (US 6, UK 8) needles and yarn A, cast on 48 sts, then ktbl to form a neat edge.

Rows 1 and 2: *k1, p1*, rep from * to * end of row.

Row 3: *k2A, k2B*, rep from * to * end of row.

Row 4: p1B *p2A, p2B*, rep from * to * last 3 sts, p2A, p1B.

Row 5: *k2B, k2A*, rep from * to * end of row.

Rows 6 and 14: p1A, *p2B, p2A*, rep from * to * last 3 sts, p2B, p1A.

Rows 7, 13 and 17: as row 3.

Rows 8, 12 and 16: as row 4.

Rows 9, 11 and 15: as row 5.

Row 10: p1A, *p2B, p2A*, rep from * to * last 3 sts, p2B, p1A.

Rep rows 1–10 of main pattern once more, then rows 1–5 of main pattern once. The next 2 rows follow the rib sequence you did in rows 1 and 2 after the initial cast on.

Row 18: using yarn A, purl.

Rows 19 and 20: using yarn B, st st.

Row 21: using yarn A, knit, increasing 1 st at both ends of the row (50 sts).

BORDER

Change to 4.5mm (US 7, UK 7) needles.

Row 1: *p5A, p2B, p1A, p2B*, rep from * to * end of row.

Row 2: *k2B, k1A, k2B, k5A*, rep from * to * end of row.

Row 3: p2A, p1B, *p4A, p1B*, rep from * to * last 2 sts, p2A.

Row 4: as row 2.

Row 5: as row 1.

Row 6: *k5A, k2B, k1A, k2B*, rep from * to * end of row.

Row 7: *p2B, p1A, p2B, p5A*, rep from * to * end of row.

Row 8: k2A, *k1B, k4A*, rep from * to * last 3 sts, k1B, k2A.

Row 9: *p2B, p1A, p2B, p5A*, rep from * to * end of row.

Row 10: as row 6.

Rep rows 1–10, then rep rows 1–5 once more. Cut off yarn B and continue using yarn A only.

Change to 4mm (US 6, UK 8) needles.

Next row: knit, decreasing 1 st at each end of row (48 sts).

Next 2 rows: k1, p1, rep from * to * end of row.

Cast off.

MAKING UP

With RS facing and using mattress stitch, join side seam 4¾in (12cm) from the wrist end and 2³⁄₈in (6cm) from the finger end. This will leave a gap for your thumb to go through. Weave in all loose ends.

This pattern was inspired by a vintage pattern that I saw. I love the muted combination of colours, but this design would work equally well in bright colours.

Unisex Headband

Materials:

» 1 ball of light worsted (DK/8-ply) yarn in self-patterning blue, grey, yellow and cream; 100g/245yd/224m

Needles:

» 4mm (US 6, UK 8) knitting needles

Instructions:

Cast on 18 sts.

Row 1 and odd-numbered rows: knit.

Row 2 and even-numbered rows: k3, purl to last 3 sts, k3.

Repeat these 2 rows until work is long enough to fit around your head when stretched slightly.

Cast off.

MAKING UP

With RS together, join seams using mattress stitch. Weave in all loose ends.

This unisex headband is very simple to make but looks more complex because of the self-patterning yarn, which creates an attractive design.

Parisienne Boot Cuffs

Materials:
- » 1 ball each of worsted (aran/10-ply) alpaca yarn in walnut (A) and black (B); 100g/144yd/132m

Needles:
- » 5mm (US 8, UK 6) knitting needles
- » 4.5mm (US 7, UK 7) knitting needles

Instructions:

Make two.

Using 4.5mm (US 7, UK 7) needles and yarn A, cast on 54 sts.

Rows 1–21: *k3, p3* rep from * to * to end of row.

Row 22: as above, increasing 1 st in 27th st (55 sts).

PATTERN

Using 5mm (US 8, UK 6) needles:

Row 1: k7, *yo, sl1, k1, psso knit st, k2, k2tog, yo, k3*, rep from * to * ending last repeat with k6.

Row 2 and all even-numbered rows: purl.

Row 3: k8, *yo, sl1, k1, psso, k2tog, yo, k5*, rep from * to * ending last repeat with k7.

Row 5: k9, *yo, sl1, k1, psso, k7*, rep from * to *, ending last repeat with k8.

Rows 6–17: rep rows 1–6 twice more.

Cut off yarn A, leaving sufficient yarn to sew up the seam.

Row 18: join in yarn B and knit to end.

PICOT POINT CAST-OFF

Cast off 2 sts *slip remaining st on right-hand needle on to left-hand needle, cast on 2 sts using cable method, cast off 4 sts*. Rep from * to * until you reach end of row. Fasten off last stitch.

MAKING UP

Weave in all loose ends. With RS facing, use mattress stitch to join the side seams of the pattern component of the boot cuff. Sew up the rib on the rear side of the boot cuff.

BOWS

Make two.

Using 5mm (US 8, UK 6) needles and yarn B, cast on 7 sts.

Row 1: p1, *k1, p1*, rep from * to * twice more.

Repeat row 1 until work measures 3¹⁄₈in (8cm). Weave in all loose ends. Take a length of yarn B and wind it round the centre of the strip to make a bow. Sew in ends and fasten the bow to the centre front of the boot cuff.

These chic boot cuffs will fit snugly into the top of boots of any length. They combine a lace effect and a picot edge to add style, and are suitable for an experienced knitter.

Cable-knit Peaked Cap

Materials:
- » 1 ball of worsted (aran/10-ply) pure wool in cream; 100g/138yd/126m
- » Piece of plastic for peak
- » 2 buttons

Tools:
- » 5mm (US 8, UK 6) circular knitting needle, 16in (40cm) long
- » 5mm (US 8, UK 6) DPN
- » Cable needle
- » Stitch marker

Gauge (tension):
- » Tension over cable pattern: 22 sts x 22 rows = 4in (10cm) square using 5mm (US 8, UK 6) needles over pattern

Instructions:

MAIN BODY

Using the circular needles, cast on 96 sts. Place a stitch marker to denote start of each round. Join the round, being careful not to twist any stitches. Slip marker as you pass it on each round.

Round 1: *k1, p1, rep from * to end of round.
Round 2: *p1, k1, rep from * to end of round.
Round 3: *k1, p1, rep from * to end of round.

Start cable pattern as follows:

Round 1: *k12, p4, rep from * to end of round.
Round 2: as round 1.
Round 3: *C6F, C6B, p4, rep from * to end of round.
Rounds 4–8: as round 2.

Rep rounds 1–8 until work measures approximately 6¾in (17cm) ending with a round 4.

SHAPING THE CROWN

Round 1: *k2tog six times, p2tog twice, rep from * to end of round (48 sts).

Change to DPN. Distribute remaining sts over 3 needles, placing your marker at the start of every round.

Round 2: *k2tog 3 times, p2tog once, rep from * to end of round (24 sts).
Rounds 3 and 4: *k3, p1 rep from * to end of round.
Round 5: *k2tog, k1, p1, rep from * to end of round (18 sts).

MAKING UP

Cut yarn and thread through rem sts. Pull yarn up tightly and fasten off. Weave in all loose ends.

PEAK

Using DPN, cast on 40 sts.
Row 1 (RS): knit 25, turn.
Row 2: slip 1, p12, turn.
Row 3: slip 1, k15, turn.
Row 4: slip 1, p18, turn.

Continue in pattern as set increasing 3 sts every row before the turn, until all 40 sts have been worked.

Work 6 rows in st st.

Cast off 2 sts at beg of next 10 rows (20 sts).

Cast off 3 sts at beg of next 4 rows (8 sts).

Cast off rem 8 sts.

Press the peak and fold it in half. Cut a piece of plastic to the shape of the peak (I used the top of a plastic biscuit box) and place inside the peak. Sew the edges of the peak together with RS facing.

STRAP

Cast on 7 sts.
Row 1: *k1, p1 rep from * to last st, k1.

Repeat row 1 until work measures approximately 10in (25cm).
Cast off.

MAKING UP

Sew the peak to the centre front of the cap, using the cables to help you to centre it. Sew the strap at either end of the peak and place and sew a button at either end of the strap. Weave in all loose ends.